Study Guide

SURVEY OF ECONOMICS
8th Edition

Irvin B. Tucker
University of North Carolina at Charlotte

SOUTH-WESTERN
CENGAGE Learning

Australia•Brazil•Japan•Korea•Mexico•Singapore•Spain•United Kingdom•United States

For product information and technology assistance, contact us at **Cengage Learning Academic Resource Center, 1-800-423-0563**.

For permission to use material from this text or product, submit all requests online at **www.cengage.com/permissions**. Further permissions questions can be emailed to **permissionrequest@cengage.com**.

ISBN-13: 978-1-133-56240-5
ISBN-10: 1-133-56240-X

South-Western Cengage Learning
5191 Natorp Boulevard
Mason, OH 45040
USA

Cengage Learning is a leading provider of customized learning solutions with office locations around the globe, including Singapore, the United Kingdom, Australia, Mexico, Brazil, and Japan. Locate your local office at: **international.cengage.com/region**.

Cengage Learning products are represented in Canada by Nelson Education, Ltd.

For your course and learning solutions, visit **www.cengage.com**.

Purchase any of our products at your local college store or at our preferred online store **www.cengagebrain.com**.

Printed in the United States of America
1 2 3 4 5   18 17 16 15 14

CONTENTS

PART IV MONEY, BANKING, AND MONETARY POLICY

PART V THE INTERNATIONAL ECONOMY

PREFACE

How to Use This Study Guide

This *Study Guide* is designed to be used with *Survey of Economics 8e* by Irvin B. Tucker. The study guide provides drill, repetition, and exercises to identify problems and prepare you for quizzes. Each chapter of the study guide contains several sections. Here are some explanations for each of these sections:

Chapter in a Nutshell and Key Concepts

The Chapter in a Nutshell provides a brief review of the important ideas in the chapter. The Key Concepts section lists the important concepts introduced in the corresponding text chapter. Before proceeding to any of the other sections, you should review each concept by defining it in your mind. If you do not understand any of the concepts, you should reread the appropriate sections in the text chapter.

The Learning Objectives

This section lists the key concepts that you will be able to understand after completing each chapter.

Economist's Tool Kit

Included in many chapters is a section called "The Economist's Tool Kit." The purpose of this feature is to reach into the economist's collection of basic models and explain each model in a clear step-by-step presentation. You will find this technique a useful supplement to the graphs in the text.

Completion Questions

After you have reviewed the key concepts, you are prepared to work through the completion questions. Each completion question's answer can be found in the key concepts section. After filling in the blanks, check yourself by the answers given at the end of the chapter. If you do not know why the answer given is the correct one, refer back to the proper section of the text.

Multiple Choice and True or False Questions

Multiple choice and true or false questions test your understanding of the basic economic concepts presented in the text chapter. Your instructor has a test bank of similar questions from which to choose exam questions. The questions in this study guide provide the types of questions that may be asked. If you have trouble with any of the multiple choice questions or true/false questions, be concerned. Go back to the text and carefully reread the discussion of the concept that is giving you a problem.

Crossword Puzzles

Crossword puzzles provide an interesting way to give you practice in the use of concepts in the chapter.

Additional Website Learning Resources

Visit the Tucker Web site at **http://cengage.com/economics/tucker/survey_of_economics8e.**

Flashcards

The key concepts for each chapter can be selected. Next, the flip card gives the definition for students to test their understanding.

Interactive Quizzes

Test your understanding of the chapter's concepts with the interactive quiz. Each quiz contains multiple questions like those found on a typical exam. Feedback is included for each answer so that you may know instantly why you have answered correctly or incorrectly. In addition, you may email yourself and/or your instructor the quiz results with a listing of correct and incorrect answers.

Practice Quizzes

A great help before quizzes. Many instructors test students using multiple-choice questions. For this reason, the final section of each chapter provides the type of multiple-choice questions given in the instructor's Test Bank. The answers to all of these questions are given in the back of the text. In addition, students may visit the Tucker Web site and answer these questions online. Here an explanation for each correct answer is given.

Online Exercises

These exercises for each chapter are designed to spark students' excitement about researching on the Internet by asking them to access online economic data and then answer questions related to the content of the chapter. All Internet exercises are on the Tucker Web site with direct links to the addresses so that students will not have the tedious and error-prone task of entering long Web site addresses.

Best of success with your course!

Irvin B. Tucker

PART I
INTRODUCTION TO ECONOMICS

Chapter 1
Introducing the Economic Way of Thinking

■ CHAPTER IN A NUTSHELL

The major objective of this chapter is to acquaint the student with the subject of economics. The birth of the Levi Strauss Company introduces the heart of economics: Economics is about people making choices concerning the allocation of scarce resources. This story highlights the success of a young entrepreneur who combined the resources of land, labor, and capital to transform canvas into a new type of pants. Another purpose of this chapter is to introduce the economic way of thinking by explaining steps in the model-building process. Economists use models and theories to focus on critical variables, such as price and quantity consumed, by abstracting from other variables that complicate the analysis. The chapter closes with a discussion of the distinction between positive economics and normative economics, which explains why economists sometimes disagree.

■ KEY CONCEPTS

Capital	Microeconomics
Ceteris paribus	Model
Economics	Normative economics
Entrepreneurship	Positive economics
Labor	Resources
Land	Scarcity
Macroeconomics	

■ LEARNING OBJECTIVES

After completing this chapter, you should be able to:

1. Understand that if there was no scarcity there would be no such thing as economics. Economics is the study of scarcity and how we deal with it.
2. Understand that scarcity exists because we are unable to produce as much as we would like (our wants are unlimited while our means of production are limited).
3. Understand that we try to do the best we can with what we have—to maximize our production with our limited resources (factors of production).
4. List the factors of production: land, labor, and capital.
5. Distinguish between "macro" and "micro."
6. Distinguish between "positive" and "normative" economic analysis.

7.   Explain why economists are interested in relationships between economic variables.
8.   Explain why theories enable us to discern relationships between economic variables.
9.   Know how theories can be expressed.
10.   Explain the limitations to the use of theories.

■ COMPLETION QUESTIONS

1.   _____ is the fundamental economic problem that human wants exceed the availability of time, goods, and resources.

2.   _____ is the study of how individuals and society choose to allocate scarce resources to satisfy unlimited wants.

3.   Factors of production classified as: land, labor, and capital are also called _____.

4.   _____ applies an economywide perspective which focuses on such issues as inflation, unemployment, and the growth rate of the economy.

5.   _____ examines small units of an economy, analyzing individual markets such as the market for personal computers.

6.   A simplified description of reality used to understand and predict economic events is called a (an) _____.

7.   If the _____ assumption is violated, a model cannot be tested.

8.   _____ uses testable statements.

9.   _____ is a shorthand expression for any natural resource provided by nature.

10.   The physical plants, machinery, and equipment used to produce other goods. Capital goods are man-made goods that do not directly satisfy human wants is _____.

11.   The mental and physical capacity of workers to produce goods and services is _____.

12.   _____ is the creative ability of individuals to seek profits by combining resources to produce innovative products.

13.   _____ is an analysis based on value judgment.

■ MULTIPLE CHOICE

1.   The condition of scarcity:

    a.   cannot be eliminated.
    b.   prevails in poor economies.
    c.   prevails in rich economies.
    d.   All of the above are true.

2.   The condition of scarcity can be eliminated if:

    a.   people satisfy needs rather than false wants.
    b.   sufficient new resources were discovered.
    c.   output of goods and services were increased.
    d.   none of the above are true.

3.   Which of the following is *not* a factor of production?

    a.   A computer chip.
    b.   The service of a lawyer.
    c.   Dollars.
    d.   All of the above are factors of production.
    e.   None of the above.

4.   A textbook is an example of:

    a.   capital.
    b.   a natural resource.
    c.   labor.
    d.   none of the above.

5.   The subject of economics is primarily the study of:

    a.   the government decision-making process.
    b.   how to operate a business successfully.
    c.   decision-making because of the problem of scarcity.
    d.   how to make money in the stock market.

6.   Which of the following is included in the study of macroeconomics?

    a.   Salaries of college professors.
    b.   Computer prices.
    c.   Unemployment in the nation.
    d.   Silver prices.

7. Microeconomics approaches the study of economics from the viewpoint of:

a. individual or specific markets.
b. the national economy.
c. government units.
d. economywide markets.

8. The definition of a model is a:

a. description of all variables affecting a situation.
b. positive analysis of all variables affecting an event.
c. simplified description of reality to understand and predict an economic event.
d. data adjusted for rational action.

9. Which of the following is a positive statement?

a. I think we should pass a constitutional amendment to reduce the deficit.
b. President Clinton's way of dealing with the economy is better than President Bush's.
c. I hope interest rates come down soon.
d. If taxes are raised, unemployment will drop.

10. "An increase in the federal minimum wage will provide a living wage for the working poor" is a:

a. statement of positive economics.
b. fallacy of composition.
c. tautology.
d. statement of normative economics.

11. Select the normative statement that completes the following sentence: If the minimum wage is raised:

a. cost per unit of output will rise.
b. workers will gain their rightful share of total income.
c. the rate of inflation will increase.
d. profits will fall.

12. "The government should provide health care for all citizens." This statement is an illustration of:

a. positive economic analysis.
b. correlation analysis.
c. fallacy of association analysis.
d. normative economic analysis.

© 2013 Cengage Learning. All Rights Reserved. May not be scanned, copied or duplicated, or posted to a publicly accessible website, in whole or in part.

13.   The software programs that make computer hardware useful in production and
        management tasks are:

        a.   capital.
        b.   labor.
        c.   a natural resource.
        d.   None of the above.

14.   An economic theory claims that a rise in gasoline prices will cause gasoline purchases
        to fall, ceteris paribus. The phrase "ceteris paribus" means that:

        a.   other relevant factors like consumer incomes must be held constant.
        b.   the gasoline prices must first be adjusted for inflation.
        c.   the theory is widely accepted but cannot be accurately tested.
        d.   consumers' need for gasoline remains the same regardless of the price.

15.   "The federal minimum wage causes higher unemployment among teenagers" is a:

        a.   statement of positive economics.
        b.   statement of normative economics.
        c.   testable value judgment.
        d.   fallacy of composition.

16.   Which of the following would eliminate scarcity as an economic problem?

        a.   Moderation of people's competitive instincts.
        b.   Discovery of sufficiently large new energy reserves.
        c.   Resumption of steady productivity growth.
        d.   None of the above.

17.   All of the following are examples of capital *except:*

        a.   the robot used to help produce your car.
        b.   a computer used by your professor to write this exam.
        c.   the factory that produces the costume jewelry you buy.
        d.   the inventory of unsold goods at your local hardware store.
        e.   an uncut diamond that you discover in your backyard.

18.   Which of the following would *not* be classified as a capital resource?

        a.   The Empire State Building.
        b.   A Caterpillar bulldozer.
        c.   A Macintosh computer.
        d.   100 shares of stock in General Motors.

19.   If a textbook price rises and then students reduce the quantity demanded of textbooks, an economic model can show a cause-and-effect relationship only if which of the following occurs?

     a.   students' incomes fall.
     b.   tuition decreases.
     c.   the number of students increases.
     d.   all other factors are held constant.
     e.   the bookstore no longer accepts used book trade-ins.

20.   Which of the following is *true* about renewable resources?

     a.   Land resources include oil, coal, and natural gas that have a fixed stock.
     b.   Land resources include irrigation networks and wastewater treatment plants that utilize water.
     c.   Land resources include air filtration systems in buildings that renew and refresh polluted air from the outside.
     d.   Land resources include forests, range lands, and marine fisheries that naturally regenerate.

■ TRUE OR FALSE

1.   T   F   All human wants cannot be satisfied because of the problem of scarcity.

2.   T   F   Economics is the study of people's making choices faced with the problem of unlimited wants and limited resources.

3.   T   F   Policies to determine the price of troll dolls are a concern of macroeconomics.

4.   T   F   Policies to increase the supply of money in the economy are primarily a concern of microeconomics.

5.   T   F   The statement "A tax hike for the rich is the fairest way to raise tax collections" is an example of positive economic analysis.

6.   T   F   The statement "The income tax is unfair to those who work hard to earn their incomes" is an example of positive economic analysis.

7.   T   F   The statement "It would be better to put up with price controls than to have continuing higher medical care prices" is an example of normative economic analysis.

8.   T   F   The statement "Cutting government spending is the best way to boost consumer confidence" is an example of normative economics.

9.   T   F   The statement "It is better to suffer a little more unemployment and a little lower prices" is an example of normative economic analysis.

10.   T   F   The statement "American workers are lazy" is an example of positive economic analysis.

■ CROSSWORD PUZZLE

Fill in the crossword puzzle from the list of key concepts. Not all of the concepts are used.

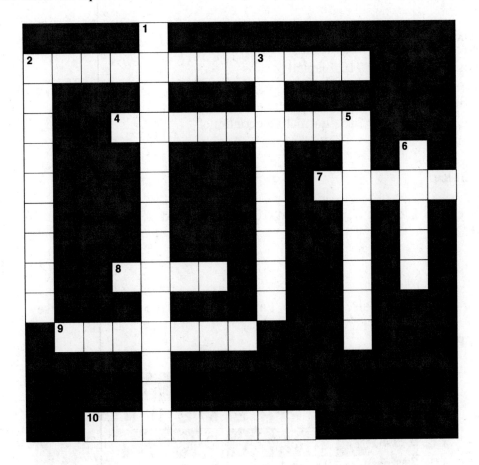

ACROSS

2.   An individual that seeks profits by combining resources to produce innovative products.
4.   The basic categories of inputs used to produce goods and services.
7.   The mental and physical capacity of workers to produce.
8.   A natural resource.
9.   Man-made goods used to produce other goods.
10.   _____ economics is an analysis limited to statements that are verifiable by reference to facts.

DOWN

1.   A phrase that means that while certain variables change, "all other things remain unchanged or constant."
2.   The study of how society chooses to allocate its scarce resources to satisfy unlimited wants.
3.   _____ economics is an analysis based on value judgement which cannot be proven by facts.
5.   The condition that human wants are forever greater than supply.
6.   A simplified description of reality.

■ ANSWERS

Completion Questions

1. scarcity
2. economics
3. resources
4. macroeconomics
5. microeconomics
6. model
7. ceteris paribus
8. positive economics
9. land
10. capital
11. labor
12. entrepreneurship
13. normative economics

Multiple Choice

1. d 2. d 3. c 4. a 5. c 6. c 7. a 8. c 9. d 10. d 11. b 12. d 13. a 14. a 15. a 16. d 17. e 18. d 19. d 20. d

True or False

1. True 2. True 3. False 4. False 5. False 6. False 7. True 8. True 9. True 10. False

Crossword Puzzle

Chapter 1A
Appendix: Applying Graphs to Economics

■ CHAPTER IN A NUTSHELL

In economics, information is best and most easily displayed by variables in a graph. If one variable rises as the other rises, the two variables are directly related. If one variable rises as the other falls, the two variables are inversely related. The slope of a line is the ratio of the change in the variable on the vertical axis to the change in the variable on the horizontal axis. An upward-sloping line represents two variables that are directly related. A downward-sloping line represents two variables that are inversely related. If one variable rises, as the other remains constant, or unchanged, the two variables are independent. Economists also use three-variable, multi-curve graphs. Using this approach, the relationship between the variables on the X and Y axis, such as price and quantity demanded, are represented by separate lines. The location of each individual line on the graph is determined by a third variable such as annual income.

■ KEY CONCEPTS

Direct relationship
Independent relationship
Inverse relationship
Slope

■ LEARNING OBJECTIVES

After completing this appendix, you should be able to:

1. Know what a direct relationship is and how it is reflected graphically.
2. Know what an inverse relationship is and how it is reflected graphically.

■ COMPLETION QUESTIONS

1. A _____ provides a means to clearly show economic relationships in a two-dimensional space.

2. A (an) _____ is one in which two variables change in the same direction.

3. A (an) _____ is one in which two variables change in the opposite direction.

4. The ratio of the vertical change (the rise or fall) to the horizontal change (the run) is called the _____.

5. A (an) _____ is one in which two variables are unrelated.

■ MULTIPLE CHOICE

Exhibit 1 Straight line

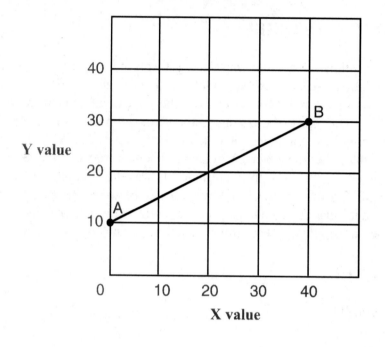

1.   Straight line AB in Exhibit 1 shows that:

   a.   increasing values for X will decrease the values of Y.
   b.   decreasing values for X will increase the values of Y.
   c.   there is a direct relationship between X and Y.
   d.   all of the above.
   e.   none of the above.

2.   In Exhibit 1, the slope of straight line AB is:

   a.   positive.
   b.   zero.
   c.   negative.
   d.   variable.

3.   In Exhibit 1, the slope of straight line AB is:

   a.   1.
   b.   5.
   c.   1/2.
   d.   -1.

4.   As shown in Exhibit 1, the slope of straight line AB:

    a.   decreases with increases in X.
    b.   increases with increases in X.
    c.   increases with decreases in X.
    d.   remains constant with changes in X.

5.   In Exhibit 1, as X increases along the horizontal axis, corresponding to points A-B on the line, the Y values increase. The relationship between the X and Y variables is:

    a.   direct.
    b.   inverse.
    c.   independent.
    d.   variable.

Exhibit 2 Straight line

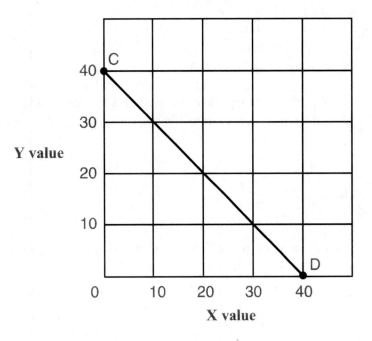

6.   Straight line CD in Exhibit 2 shows that:

    a.   increasing values for X increases the value of Y.
    b.   decreasing values for X decreases the value of Y.
    c.   there is an inverse relationship between X and Y.
    d.   all of the above.
    e.   none of the above.

7.   In Exhibit 2, the slope of straight line CD is:

    a.   positive.
    b.   zero.
    c.   negative.
    d.   variable.

8.   In Exhibit 2, the slope for straight line CD is:

    a.   5.
    b.   1.
    c.   -1.
    d.   -5.

9.   As shown in Exhibit 2, the slope of straight line CD:

    a.   decreases with increases in X.
    b.   increases with increases in X.
    c.   increases with decreases in X.
    d.   remains constant with changes in X.

10.   In Exhibit 2, as X increases along the horizontal axis, corresponding to points C-D on the line, the Y values decrease. The relationship between the X and Y variables is:

    a.   direct.
    b.   inverse.
    c.   independent.
    d.   variable.

11.   In Exhibit 2, if the slope of line CD were zero, the relationship between the X and Y variable is:

    a.   direct.
    b.   inverse.
    c.   independent.
    d.   variable.

Exhibit 3 Straight line

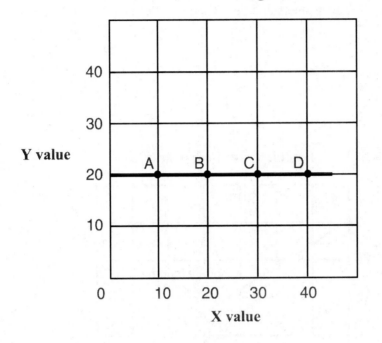

12.   Straight line A-D in Exhibit 3 shows that:

a.   increasing value for X will increase the value of Y.
b.   increasing value for X will decrease the value of Y.
c.   increasing values for X do not affect the value of Y.
d.   all of the above.
e.   none of the above.

13.   In Exhibit 3, the slope of straight line A-D is:

a.   positive.
b.   zero.
c.   negative.
d.   variable.

14.   In Exhibit 3, the slope of the straight line A-D is:

a.   0.
b.   1.
c.   1/2.
d.   -1.

15.   In Exhibit 3, as X increases along the horizontal axis, corresponding to points A-D on the line, the Y values remain unchanged at 20 units. The relationship between the X and Y variables is:

    a.   direct.
    b.   inverse.
    c.   independent.
    d.   undefined.

Exhibit 4 Multi-curve graph

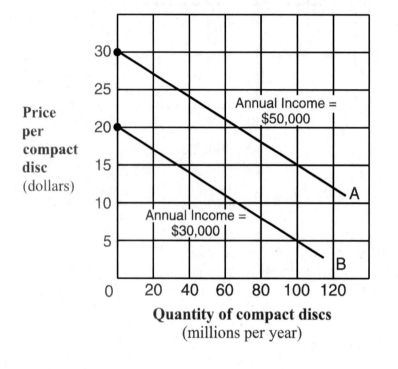

16.   Exhibit 4 represents a three-variable relationship. As the annual income of consumers falls from $50,000 (line A) to $30,000 (line B), the result is a (an):

    a.   upward movement along each curve.
    b.   downward movement along each curve.
    c.   leftward shift in curve A.
    d.   rightward shift in curve B.

17.   Measured between two points on a curve, the ratio of the change in the variable on the vertical axis to the change in the variable on the horizontal axis is the:

    a.   axis.
    b.   slope.
    c.   dependent curve.
    d.   independent curve.

18.   A line that has a different slope at each point is s:

    a.   curve.
    b.   straight line.
    c.   vertical line.
    d.   horizontal line.

19.   In a graphic relationship, shifts in a curve are caused by a change in:

    a.   the slope of the curve.
    b.   a factor not measured on the axes of the graph.
    c.   one of the factors measured on either axes of the graph.
    d.   any factor, whether measured on the axes of the graph or not.

20.   A change in a third variable *not* on either axis of a graph is illustrated with a:

    a.   horizontal or vertical line.
    b.   movement along a curve.
    c.   shift of a curve.
    d.   point of intersection.

■ ANSWERS

Completion Questions

1. graph
2. direct relationship
3. inverse relationship
4. slope
5. independent relationship

Multiple Choice

1. c 2. a 3. c 4. d 5. a 6. c 7. c 8. c 9. d 10. b 11. c 2. c 13. b 14. a 15. c 16. c 17. b 18. a 19. b 20. c

Chapter 2
Production Possibilities, Opportunity Cost, and Economic Growth

■ CHAPTER IN A NUTSHELL

In this chapter, you continue your quest to learn the economic way of thinking. The chapter begins with the three basic questions each economy must answer: (1) What to produce? (2) How to produce? and (3) For whom to produce? The chapter then introduces concepts which economists use to analyze choice-the production possibilities curve and opportunity costs. The production possibilities curve indicates various maximum combinations of the output of two goods a simple economy can produce. The economy can achieve economic growth by pushing the production possibilities curve outward. This shift in the curve can be caused by increasing resources and/or advances in technology.

■ KEY CONCEPTS

Economic growth
Investment
Law of increasing opportunity
   costs
Marginal analysis
New economy

Opportunity cost
Production possibilities curve
Technology
What, How, and
   For Whom questions

■ LEARNING OBJECTIVES

After completing this chapter, you should be able to:

1. Explain how capitalism answers the "What", "How", and "For Whom" fundamental economic questions.
2. Understand what is meant by an opportunity cost and give some examples.
3. Explain why an opportunity cost is an implicit cost incurred in making all decisions.
4. Explain why marginal analysis can give rise to more rational decisions.
5. Graphically express a production possibilities model.
6. Understand that the production possibilities model illustrates the problem of scarcity, therefore choices have to made, and when choices are made that an opportunity cost is incurred.
7. Illustrate production efficiency and inefficiency in the context of the production possibilities graph.
8. Describe what is meant by the law of increasing opportunity cost and why it exists.
9. Explain what is meant by investment.
10. Explain why a nation's decision to invest and produce more capital goods now will increase the nation's rate of economic growth over time.
11. Illustrate and explain economic growth in the context of a production possibilities model.

THE ECONOMIST'S TOOL KIT
Plotting the Production Possibilities Curve

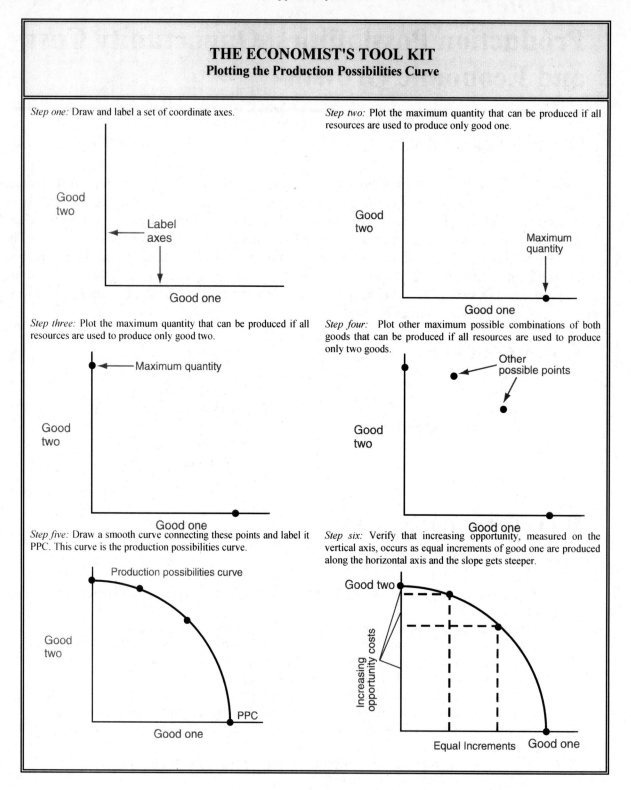

Step one: Draw and label a set of coordinate axes.

Step two: Plot the maximum quantity that can be produced if all resources are used to produce only good one.

Step three: Plot the maximum quantity that can be produced if all resources are used to produce only good two.

Step four: Plot other maximum possible combinations of both goods that can be produced if all resources are used to produce only two goods.

Step five: Draw a smooth curve connecting these points and label it PPC. This curve is the production possibilities curve.

Step six: Verify that increasing opportunity, measured on the vertical axis, occurs as equal increments of good one are produced along the horizontal axis and the slope gets steeper.

■ COMPLETION QUESTIONS

1.   The _____ problem concerns the division of output among society's citizens. The _____ question asks exactly which goods are to be produced and in what quantities. The _____ question requires society to decide the resource mix used to produce goods.

2.   _____ is the best alternative forgone for a chosen option.

3.   The basic approach that compares additional benefits of a change against the additional costs of the change is called _____.

4.   The _____ represents the maximum possible combinations of two outputs that can be produced in a given period of time. Inefficient production occurs at any point inside the curve and all points along the curve are efficient points.

5.   The _____ states that the opportunity cost increases as production of an output expands.

6.   _____ occurs when the production possibilities curve shifts outward as the result of changes in the resource base or advance in technology.

7.   Factories, equipment, and inventories produced in the present are called _____which can be used to shift the production possibilities curve outward in the future.

8.   The body of knowledge and skills applied to how goods are produced is _____.

■ MULTIPLE CHOICE

1.   Which of the following is *not* one of the three fundamental economic questions?

    a.   What happens when you add to or subtract from a current situation?
    b.   For whom to produce?
    c.   How to produce?
    d.   What to produce?

2.   Which of the following does *not* illustrate opportunity cost?

    a.   If I study, I must give up going to the football game.
    b.   If I buy a computer, I must do without a 35" television.
    c.   *More* consumer spending now means *more* spending in the future.
    d.   If I spend more on clothes, I must spend less on food.

3.   Which of the following would be *most* likely to cause the production possibilities curve for computers and education to shift outward?

   a.   A choice of more computers and less education.
   b.   A choice of more education and less computers.
   c.   A reduction in the labor force.
   d.   An increase in the quantity of resources.

Exhibit 1 Production possibilities curve data

	A	B	C	D	E	F
Capital goods	15	14	12	9	5	0
Consumer goods	0	2	4	6	8	10

4.   As shown in Exhibit 1, the concept of increasing opportunity costs is reflected in the fact that:

   a.   the quantity of consumer goods produced can never be zero.
   b.   the labor force in the economy is homogeneous.
   c.   greater amounts of capital goods must be sacrificed to produce an additional 2 units of consumer goods.
   d.   a graph of the production data is a downward-sloping straight line.

5.   As shown in Exhibit 1, a total output of 0 units of capital goods and 10 units of consumer goods is:

   a.   the maximum possible output of capital goods for this economy.
   b.   an inefficient way of using the economy's scarce resources.
   c.   the result of efficient use of the economy's resources.
   d.   unobtainable in this economy.

6.   As shown in Exhibit 1, a total output of 14 units of capital goods and 0 units of consumer goods is:

   a.   the result of maximum use of the economy's labor force.
   b.   an efficient way of using the economy's scarce resources.
   c.   unobtainable in this economy.
   d.   less than the maximum rate of output for this economy.

Exhibit 2 Production possibilities curve

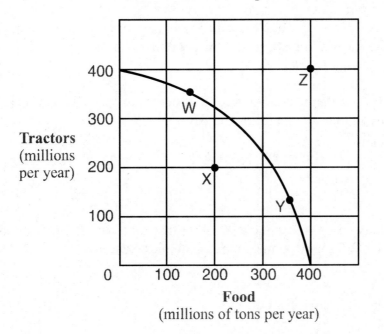

7.   If the economy represented in Exhibit 2 is operating at Point W:

    a.   no tractor production must be forgone to produce more food in the current period.
    b.   resources are not fully used.
    c.   some tractor production must be forgone to produce more food in the current period.
    d.   increased food production would be impossible.

8.   Which of the following moves from one point to another in Exhibit 2 would represent an increase in economic efficiency?

    a.   Z to W.
    b.   W to Y.
    c.   W to X.
    d.   X to Y.

9.   Movement along this production possibilities curve shown in Exhibit 2 indicates:

    a.   that labor is not equally productive or homogeneous.
    b.   declining opportunity costs.
    c.   all inputs are homogeneous.
    d.   all of the above.

10.   In order for the economy shown in Exhibit 2 to reach point Z, it must:

   a.   suffer resource unemployment.
   b.   experience an increase in its resources and/or an improvement in its technology.
   c.   use its resources more efficiently than at point W or Y.
   d.   all of the above.

11.   The following two alternatives exist for a student who has one evening in which to prepare for two exams on the following day:

Possibility	Score in Economics	Score in Accounting
A	95	80
B	80	90

   The opportunity cost of receiving a 90 rather than an 80 on the accounting exam is represented by how many points on the economics exam?

   a.   15 points.
   b.   80 points.
   c.   90 points.
   d.   10 points.

12.   On a production possibilities curve, a change from economic inefficiency to economic efficiency is obtained by:

   a.   movement along the curve.
   b.   movement from outside the frontier to a point on the curve.
   c.   movement from a point inside the frontier to a point on the curve.
   d.   a change in the slope of the curve.

13.   One of the assumptions underlying the production possibilities curve for any given economy is that:

   a.   the state of technology is changing.
   b.   there is an unlimited supply of available resources.
   c.   there is full employment and no underemployment of resources when the economy is operating on the curve.
   d.   goods can be produced in unlimited quantities.

14.   Any point on the production possibilities curve illustrates:

   a.   minimum production combinations.
   b.   maximum production combinations.
   c.   economic growth.
   d.   a nonfeasible production combination.

15.   A production possibilities curve has "good X" on the horizontal axis and "good Y" on the vertical axis. On this diagram, the opportunity cost of good X, in terms of good Y, is represented by the:

    a.   distance to the curve from the horizontal axis.
    b.   distance to curve from the vertical axis.
    c.   movement along the curve.
    d.   none of the above.

16.   As production of a good increases, opportunity costs rise because:

    a.   there will be more inefficiency.
    b.   people always prefer having more goods.
    c.   of inflationary pressures.
    d.   workers are not equally suited to all tasks.

17.   Which of the following would be *most* likely to cause the production possibility curve for tanks and cars to shift outward?

    a.   A reduction in the labor force.
    b.   A choice of more tanks and fewer cars.
    c.   A choice of more cars and fewer tanks.
    d.   An increase in the quantity of natural resources.

18.   Which of the following cause(s) economic growth?

    a.   c and d.
    b.   d and e.
    c.   The production of more scarce goods.
    d.   A technological improvement.
    e.   The production of more capital goods.

19.   A source of economic growth is:

    a.   unemployment.
    b.   inefficiency.
    c.   less resources.
    d.   greater entrepreneurship.

20.   Investment refers to the process of accumulating:

    a.   capital goods.
    b.   consumer goods.
    c.   money.
    d.   stocks and bonds.

■ TRUE OR FALSE

1.   T   F   The opportunity cost of a good is the good or service forgone for a chosen good or service.

2.   T   F   If some resources were used inefficiently, the economy would tend to operate outside its production possibilities curve.

3.   T   F   Of all the points on the production possibilities curve, only one point represents an efficient division of labor.

4.   T   F   The most efficient point on the production possibilities curve is the midpoint on the curve.

5.   T   F   On the production possibilities curve, a movement between points that yields a loss of one good in order to raise the output of another good will maintain efficient production.

6.   T   F   If more of one good can be produced without loss of output of another along the same production possibilities curve, the economy must have been operating efficiently.

7.   T   F   All points on the production possibilities curve represent efficient levels of production.

8.   T   F   Investment is an economic term for the act of increasing the stock of money available for business loans.

9.   T   F   What to produce, how to produce, and for who to produce are the three fundamental economic questions.

10.   T   F   Unemployment or underemployment of labor might explain why an economy would be operating inside its production possibilities curve (PPC).

■ CROSSWORD PUZZLE

Fill in the crossword puzzle from the list of key concepts. Not all of the concepts are used.

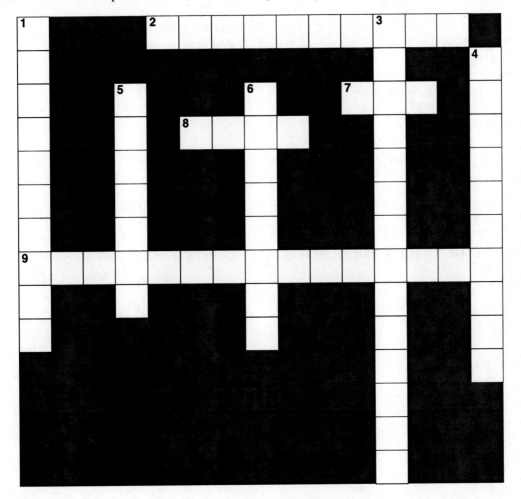

ACROSS

2. The accumulation of capital.
7. The basic economic question of which resources to use in production.
8. The basic economic question of which goods and services to produce.
9. The best alternative sacrificed.

DOWN

1. The application of knowledge to production.
3. An outward shift of the production possibilities curve.
4. The _____ possibilities curve shows the maximum combinations of two outputs than an economy can produce, given its available resources and technology.
5. The basic economic question of who receives goods and services.
6. _____ analysis means additions to or subtractions from a current situation.

■ ANSWERS

Completion Questions

1. for whom, what, how
2. opportunity cost
3. marginal analysis
4. production possibilities curve
5. law of increasing opportunity costs

6. economic growth
7. investment
8. technology

Multiple Choice

1. d 2. c 3. d 4. c 5. c 6. d 7. c 8. d 9. a 10. b 11. a 12. c 13. c 14. b 15. c 16. d 17. d 18. b 19. d 20. a

True or False

1. True 2. False 3. False 4. False 5. True 6. False 7. True 8. False 9. True 10. True

Crossword Puzzle

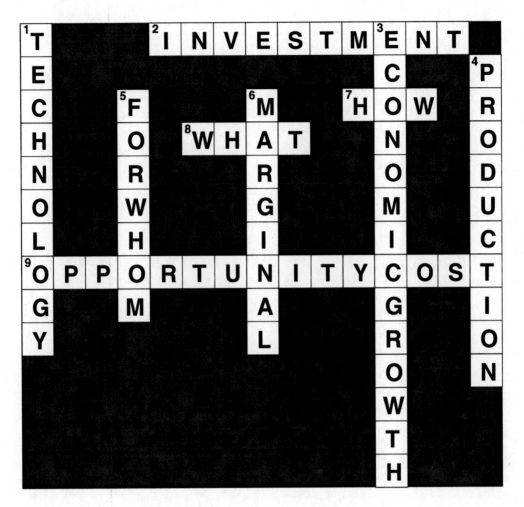

PART II
THE MICROECONOMY

Chapter 3
Market Demand and Supply

■ CHAPTER IN A NUTSHELL

Understanding the price system is a crucial milestone on your quest to learn the economic way of thinking and analyze real-world economic issues. There are two sides to a market: the market demand curve and the market supply curve. The location of the demand curve shifts when changes occur in such nonprice factors as: the number of buyers, tastes and preferences, income, expectations, and the prices of related goods. The location of the supply curve shifts when changes occur in such nonprice factors as: the number of sellers, technology, resource prices, taxes and subsidies, expectations, and prices of other goods. Ceteris paribus, the intersection of the market demand and supply curves determines the equilibrium price and equilibrium quantity of goods.

■ KEY CONCEPTS

Change in demand	Equilibrium	Price system
Change in quantity demanded	Inferior good	Shortage
Change in quantity supplied	Law of demand	Substitute good
Change in supply	Law of supply	Supply
Complementary good	Market	Surplus
Demand	Normal good	

■ LEARNING OBJECTIVES

After completing this chapter, you should be able to:

1. Describe the laws of demand and supply and express them graphically.
2. Distinguish a change in quantity demanded (supplied) from a change in demand (supply).
3. Understand that a change in the quantity demanded (supplied) is reflected graphically as movement along a given demand (supply) curve, whereas a change in demand (supply) is reflected as a complete shift of the demand (supply) curve.
4. Express an increase in demand (supply) as a rightward shift and a decrease in demand (supply) as a leftward shift of the demand (supply) curve.
5. Describe what could cause an increase and a decrease in demand (supply).
6. Graphically express market equilibrium.
7. Understand that equilibrium exists at that price in which the quantity demanded equals the quantity supplied.

8.   Graphically express a surplus and a shortage.
9.   Understand that a surplus (shortage) exists whenever the price is above (below) equilibrium and the quantity supplied exceeds (is less than) the quantity demanded.
10. Explain why a surplus (shortage) will cause the price to fall (rise) in the market.

THE ECONOMIST'S TOOL KIT
Finding the Equilibrium Price and Quantity

Step one: Label the vertical axis as the price per unit of the good or service and the horizontal axis as the quantity of the good or service per time period. Draw a downward-sloping demand curve and label it D. Draw an upward-sloping supply curve and label it S. Label the price where the quantity demanded equals the quantity supplied as P^* and the corresponding quantity as Q^*.

Step two: Choose a price above the equilibrium price and label it P_1. Note that the quantity demanded Q_D is less than the quantity supplied Q_S and there is a surplus. The size of the surplus is the horizontal dotted line between Q_D and Q_S.

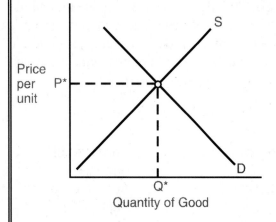

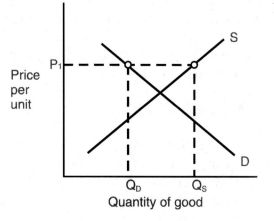

Step three: Choose a price below the equilibrium price and label it P_2. Note that the quantity supplied Q_S is less than the quantity demanded Q_D and there is a shortage. The size of the shortage is the horizontal dotted line between Q_S and Q_D.

Step four: Note that in a price system without government interference the conditions of surplus and shortage drawn above is only temporary. After a trial-and-error period of time the forces of surplus and shortage will automatically restore the equilibrium price and quantity as originally drawn in step one.

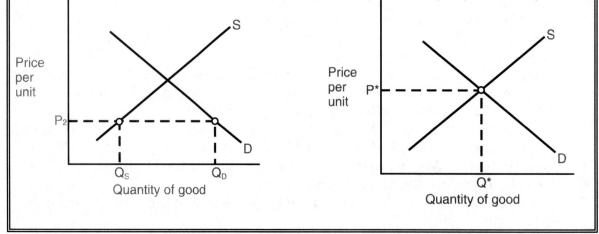

■ COMPLETION QUESTIONS

1. The _____ states that there is an inverse relationship between the price and the quantity demanded, ceteris paribus.

2. A movement along a stationary demand curve caused by a change in price is called a (an) _____.

3. A (an) _____ is one that consumers buy more of when their income increases.

4. _____ states that there is a direct relationship between the price and the quantity supplied, ceteris paribus.

5. A movement along a stationary supply curve in response to a change in price is called a (an) _____.

6. When the price of a good is greater than the equilibrium price, there is an excess quantity supplied called a (an) _____.

7. The unique price and quantity established at the intersection of the supply and demand curves is called _____.

8. The _____ is the supply and demand mechanism which establishes equilibrium through the ability of prices to rise and fall.

9. A (an) _____ is one that there is an inverse relationship between changes in income and its demand curve.

10. A (an) _____ is one that competes with another good for consumer purchases. As a result, there is a direct relationship between a price change for one good and the demand for its "competitor" good.

11. The principle that there is a direct relationship between the price of a good and the quantity sellers are willing to offer for sale in a defined time period, ceteris paribus, is the _____.

12. A (an) _____ is any arrangement in which buyers and sellers interact to determine the price and quantity of goods and services exchanged.

13. A (an) _____ is one that is jointly consumed with another good. As a result, there is an inverse relationship between a price change for one good and the demand for its "go together" good.

14. A market condition existing at any price where the quantity supplied is less than the quantity demanded is a (an) _____.

■ MULTIPLE CHOICE

1.   Which of the following is *true* for the law of demand?

   a.   Sellers increase the quantity of a good available as the price of the good increases.
   b.   An increase in price results from false needs.
   c.   There is an inverse relationship between the price of a good and the quantity of the good demanded.
   d.   Prices increase as more units of a product are demanded.

2.   A demand curve for The Steel Porcupines concert tickets would show the:

   a.   quality of service that customers demand when they buy a ticket.
   b.   number of people who like to attend the concert.
   c.   number of tickets the promoters are willing to sell at each price.
   d.   number of concert tickets that will be purchased at each price.

3.   Other things being equal, the effects of an increase in the price of computers would best be represented by which of the following?

   a.   A movement up along the demand curve for computers.
   b.   A movement down along the demand curve for computers.
   c.   A leftward shift in the demand curve for computers.
   d.   A rightward shift in the demand curve for computers.

4.   Which of the following *best* represents the effects of a decrease in the price of tomato juice, other things being equal?

   a.   An upward movement along the demand curve for tomato juice.
   b.   A downward movement along the demand curve for tomato juice.
   c.   A rightward shift in the demand curve for tomato juice.
   d.   A leftward shift in the demand curve for tomato juice.

5.   The "ceteris paribus" clause in the law of demand does not allow which of the following factors to change?

   a.   Consumer tastes and preferences.
   b.   The prices of other goods.
   c.   Expectations.
   d.   All of the above.

6.   Assume that Coca-Cola and Pepsi-Cola are substitutes. A rise in the price of Coca-Cola will have which of the following effects on the market for Pepsi?

   a.   A movement down along the Pepsi demand curve.
   b.   A rightward shift in the Pepsi demand curve.
   c.   A movement up along the Pepsi demand curve.
   d.   A leftward shift in the Pepsi demand curve.

7. Assume that crackers and soup are complementary goods. The effect on the soup market of an increase in the price of crackers (other things being equal) would best be described as a (an):

   a. decrease in the quantity of soup demanded.
   b. decrease in the demand for soup.
   c. increase in the quantity of soup demanded.
   d. increase in the demand for soup.

8. Assume that a computer is a normal good. An increase in consumer income, other things being equal, would:

   a. cause an upward movement along the demand curve for computers.
   b. cause a downward movement along the demand curve for computers.
   c. shift the demand curve for computers to the left.
   d. shift the demand curve for computers to the right.

9. Which of the following will increase the demand for large automobiles?

   a. A fall in the price of small automobiles.
   b. A rise in insurance rates for large automobiles.
   c. A fall in the price of large automobiles.
   d. An increase in buyers' incomes (assuming large automobiles to be a normal good).

10. Assume that brand X is an inferior good and name brand Y is a normal good. An increase in consumer income, other things being equal, will cause a (an):

    a. upward movement along the demand curve for name brand Y.
    b. downward movement along the demand curve for brand X.
    c. rightward shift in the demand curve for brand X.
    d. leftward shift in the demand curve for brand X.

11. There is news that the price of Tucker's Root Beer will increase significantly next week. If the demand for Tucker's Root Beer reacts *only* to this factor and shifts to the right, the position of this demand curve has reacted to a change in:

    a. tastes.
    b. income levels.
    c. the price of other goods.
    d. the number of buyers.
    e. expectations.

12.   The theory of supply states that:

a.   there is a negative relationship between the price of a good and the quantity of it purchased by suppliers.
b.   there is a positive relationship between the price of a good and the quantity that buyers choose to purchase.
c.   there is a positive relationship between the price of a good and the quantity of it offered for sale by suppliers.
d.   at a lower price, a greater quantity will be supplied.

13.   Supply curves slope upward because:

a.   the quality is assumed to vary with price.
b.   technology improves over time, increasing the ability of firms to produce more at each possible price.
c.   increases in the price of a good lead to rightward shifts of the supply curve.
d.   rising prices provide producers with higher profit incentives needed to increase the quantity supplied.

14.   Which of the following will *not* cause a movement along the supply curve?

a.   Changes in the sellers' expectations.
b.   Increases in taxes per unit of output.
c.   Advances in technology.
d.   All of the above.

15.   Assume that oranges and peaches can both be grown on the same type of land, a decrease in the price of peaches, other things being equal, will cause a (an):

a.   upward movement along the supply curve for oranges.
b.   downward movement along the supply curve for oranges.
c.   rightward shift of the supply curve for oranges.
d.   leftward shift of the supply curve for oranges.

16.   An advance in technology results in:

a.   suppliers offering a larger quantity than before at each given price.
b.   suppliers offering the same quantity as before at a lower price.
c.   a rightward shift of the supply curve.
d.   an increase in supply.
e.   all of the above.

Exhibit 1 Supply for Tucker's Cola data

Quantity supplied per week (millions of gallons)	Price per gallon
6	$3.00
5	2.50
4	2.00
3	1.50
2	1.00
1	.50

17.   As shown in Exhibit 1, the price and quantity supplied by sellers of Tucker's Cola have a (an)_____ relationship.

a.   direct.
b.   inverse.
c.   negative.
d.   zero.

18.   In reference to Exhibit 1, assume the price of Tucker's Cola is $1.00 per gallon. If the price were to rise to $3.00 per gallon, and all other factors, such as taxes, etc. remained constant, the result would be a (an):

a.   decrease in supply.
b.   increase in supply.
c.   decrease in quantity supplied.
d.   increase in quantity supplied.

19.   Assume Congress passes a new tax of $2.00 per pack on cigarettes. The effect on the supply curve is a (an):

a.   decrease in supply.
b.   increase in supply.
c.   decrease in quantity supplied.
d.   increase in quantity supplied.

20.   Market equilibrium is defined as:

a.   the condition in which there is neither a shortage or surplus.
b.   the condition under which the separately formulated plans of buyers and sellers exactly mesh when tested in the market.
c.   represented graphically by the intersection of the supply and demand curves.
d.   all of the above.

21.   Which of the following best explains the determination of the equilibrium price of a product?

    a.   Production costs.
    b.   The supply of a good.
    c.   The interaction of supply and demand.
    d.   The decisions of government.

22.   When the price of a good in a market is above equilibrium:

    a.   the quantity supplied exceeds the quantity demanded.
    b.   a surplus is observed.
    c.   the price will fall in the near future.
    d.   all of the above.

Exhibit 2 Supply and demand curves

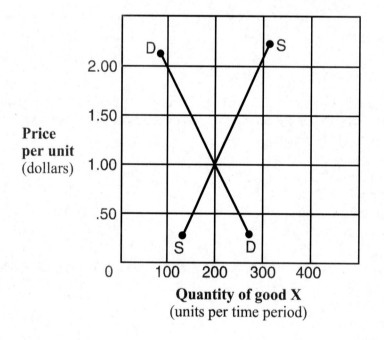

23.   In the market shown in Exhibit 2, the equilibrium price and quantity of good X are:

    a. $0.50, 250.
    b. $2.00, 300.
    c. $2.00, 100.
    d. $1.00, 200.

24.   In Exhibit 2, at a price of $.50 the market for good X will experience a:

    a.   shortage of 100 units.
    b.   surplus of 100 units.
    c.   shortage of 300 units.
    d.   surplus of 200 units.

25.   In Exhibit 2, if the price moves from $2.00 to $1.00, inventories will:

    a.   remain unchanged.
    b.   fall.
    c.   rise.
    d.   fall and then rise.

26.   In Exhibit 2, if the market price of good X is initially $.50, a movement toward equilibrium requires:

    a.   no change, because an equilibrium already exists.
    b.   the price to fall below $.50 and both the quantity supplied and the quantity demanded to rise.
    c.   the price to remain the same, but the supply curve to shift to the left.
    d.   the price to rise above $.50, the quantity supplied to rise, and the quantity demanded to fall.

27.   In Exhibit 2, if the market price of good X is initially $1.50, a movement toward equilibrium requires:

    a.   no change, because an equilibrium already exists.
    b.   the price to fall below $1.50 and both the quantity supplied and the quantity demanded to fall.
    c.   the price to remain the same, but the supply curve to shift to the left.
    d.   the price to fall below $1.50, the quantity supplied to fall, and the quantity demanded to rise.

28.   Three of the four events described below might reasonably be expected to shift the demand curve for beef to a new position. One would *not shift* the demand curve. The single exception is:

    a.   a change in people's tastes with respect to beef.
    b.   an increase in the money income of beef consumers.
    c.   a fall in the price of beef.
    d.   a widespread advertising campaign undertaken by the producers of a product competitive with beef (e.g., pork).

29.   Yesterday Seller A supplied 400 units of a good X at $10 per unit. Today Seller A supplies the same quantity of units at $5 per unit. Based on this evidence, Seller A has experienced a (an):

   a.   decrease in supply.
   b.   increase in supply.
   c.   increase in the quantity supplied.
   d.   decrease in the quantity supplied.
   e.   increase in demand.

30.   Assuming that wheat and corn can both be grown on the same type of land, a decrease in the price of corn, other factors held constant, will cause a (an):

   a.   downward movement along the supply curve for wheat.
   b.   upward movement along the supply curve for wheat.
   c.   rightward shift in the supply curve for wheat.
   d.   leftward shift in the supply curve for wheat.

■ TRUE OR FALSE

1.   T   F   According to the law of demand, if the price of a good increases, other things being equal, the quantity demanded will decrease.

2.   T   F   Other things being equal, an increase in the price of aspirin will decrease the demand for aspirin.

3.   T   F   If a vacation in Paris is a normal good, other things being equal, an increase in consumer income will increase the demand for travel to Paris.

4.   T   F   If people buy more of a generic brand when consumer income falls, it is an inferior good.

5.   T   F   If pork and beans is an inferior good, other things being equal, an increase in consumer income will decrease the demand for pork and beans.

6.   T   F   Suppose A and B are substitute goods. Other things being equal, the demand curve for A will shift to the right when the price of B goes down.

7.   T   F   Suppose A and B are complementary goods. Other things being equal, the demand curve for A will shift to the right when the price of B goes up.

8.   T   F   If input prices increase, the supply curve for cheese will shift to the right.

9.   T   F   Suppose the market price of a good X is below the equilibrium price. The result is a shortage and sellers can be expected to decrease the quantity of that good X supplied.

10.   T   F   A shortage means that the quantity demanded is greater than the quantity supplied at the prevailing price.

11.   T   F   Excess quantity demanded for a good creates pressure to push the price of that good down toward the equilibrium price.

12.   T   F   A surplus means that the quantity supplied is greater than the quantity demanded at the prevailing price.

■ CROSSWORD PUZZLE

Fill in the crossword puzzle from the list of key concepts. Not all of the concepts are used.

ACROSS

2. The principle that there is a direct relationship between the price of a good and the quantity sellers are willing to offer for sale in a defined time period, ceteris paribus.
4. Any price where the quantity demanded equals the quantity supplied.
5. A competing good.
6. A jointly consumed good.
7. When the quantity demanded exceeds the quantity supplied.
8. A change in the quantity _____ is a movement between points along a stationary demand curve, ceteris paribus.

DOWN

1. A good for which there is an inverse relationship between a change in income and its and its demand curve.
3. A mechanism that creates market equilibrium.
5. A change in the quantity _____ is a movement along a stationary supply curve, ceteris paribus.

■ ANSWERS

Completion Questions

1. law of demand
2. change in quantity demanded
3. normal good
4. law of supply
5. change in quantity supplied
6. surplus
7. equilibrium
8. price system
9. inferior good
10. substitute good
11. law of supply
12. market
13. complementary good
14. shortage

Multiple Choice

1. c 2. d 3. a 4. b 5. d 6. b 7. b 8. d 9. d 10. d 11. e 12. c 13. d 14. d 15. c 16. e 17. a
18. d 19. a 20. d 21. e 22. c 23. d 24. a 25. b 26. d 27. d 28. c 29. b 30. c

True or False

1. True 2. False 3. True 4. True 5. True 6. False 7. False 8. False 9. False 10. True 11. False 12. True

Crossword Puzzle

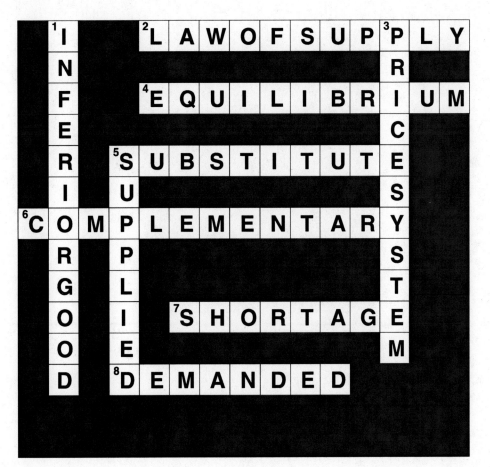

Chapter 4
Markets in Action

■ **CHAPTER IN A NUTSHELL**

Chapter 4 builds on the basic supply and demand model introduced in the previous chapter. Here the focus is on how equilibrium prices and quantities change when other factors change. Applications in the chapter, for example, to Caribbean cruises, video rentals, lumber, and oat bran are included to help you understand and appreciate the basics of supply and demand analysis. This chapter also explains what happens when the government sets price floors or ceilings and therefore prices do not adjust to the equilibrium price. The chapter concludes with an introduction to the concept of market failure that is concerned with how the price system functions when it fails. Four cases of market failure discussed are: lack of competition, externalities, public goods, and income inequality.

■ **KEY CONCEPTS**

Externality
Market failure
Price ceiling

Price floor
Public good

■ **LEARNING OBJECTIVES**

After completing this chapter, you should be able to:

1. Express graphically an increase in demand (supply) as a rightward shift and a decrease in demand (supply) as a leftward shift of the demand (supply) curve.
2. Interpret what is meant by an increase in demand (supply) or a decrease in demand (supply).
3. Explain and determine the impact of an increase or a decrease in demand (supply) on the equilibrium price and quantity using words and a graph.
4. Explain and determine the impact of a price ceiling and a price support using words and a graph.
5. List some examples of a price ceiling and a price support.
6. Describe what is meant by a market failure, list the different types, and how government has attempted to correct each of them.

THE ECONOMIST'S TOOL KIT
Comparing the Effects of Changes in Demand and Supply

Step one: Increase demand and note that both the equilibrium price and quantity increase.

Step two: Decrease demand and note that both the equilibrium price and quantity decrease.

Step three: Increase supply and note that the equilibrium price decreases and the equilibrium quantity increases.

Step four: Decrease supply and note that the equilibrium price increases and the equilibrium quantity decreases.

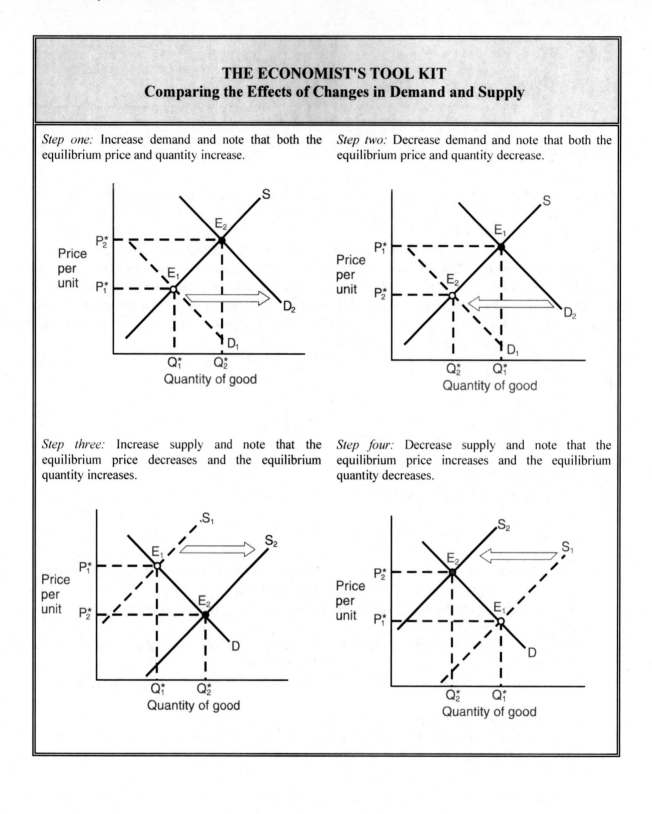

■ COMPLETION QUESTIONS

1.   A (an) _____ is a maximum price mandated by government.

2.   A (an) _____ is a minimum legal price mandated by government.

3.   Pollution is an example of _____ , which means too many resources are used to produce the product responsible for the pollution. Two basic approaches to solve this market failure are regulation and pollution taxes.

4.   Vaccination shots provide _____ which means sellers devote too few resources to produce this product. Two basic solutions to this type of market failure are laws to require consumption of shots and special subsidies.

5.   A (an) _____ is consumed by everyone regardless of whether they pay for them or not. National defense and air traffic control are examples.

6.   _____ means the price system fails to efficiently allocate resources in the production of output.

7.   A (an) _____ is a cost or benefit imposed on people other than the consumers and producers of a good or service.

■ MULTIPLE CHOICE

Exhibit 1 Supply and demand curves

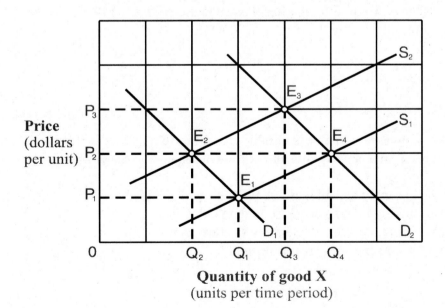

1.   Initially the market shown in Exhibit 1 is in equilibrium at P2, Q2 (E2). Changes in market conditions result in a new equilibrium at P2, Q4 (E4). This change is stated as a (an):

    a.   increase in supply and an increase in demand.
    b.   increase in supply and a decrease in demand.
    c.   decrease in demand and a decrease in supply.
    d.   increase in demand and an increase in quantity supplied.

2.   Initially the market shown in Exhibit 1 is in equilibrium at P_3, Q_3 (E_3). Changes in market conditions result in a new equilibrium at P_2, Q_2 (E_2). This change is stated as a (an):

    a.   decrease in demand and an increase in supply.
    b.   decrease in demand and a decrease in quantity supplied.
    c.   decrease in quantity demanded and an increase in quantity supplied.
    d.   decrease in quantity demanded and an increase in supply.

3.   In Exhibit 1, which of the following would *not* cause a shift from S_1 to S_2?

    a.   An increase in input prices.
    b.   A rise in the price of other goods.
    c.   An increase in taxes per unit.
    d.   An increase in consumer income.

4.   The market shown in Exhibit 1 is initially in equilibrium at point E_4. Union negotiations result in a wage increase. Other things being equal, which of the following is the new equilibrium after this wage increase is in effect?

    a. E_1.
    b. E_2.
    c. E_3.
    d. E_4.

5.   The market shown in Exhibit 1 is initially in equilibrium at E_4. Changes in market conditions result in a new equilibrium at E_3. This change is stated as a (an):

    a.   increase in supply and an increase in quantity demanded.
    b.   increase in supply and a decrease in demand.
    c.   decrease in supply and a decrease in quantity demanded.
    d.   increase in demand an increase in supply.

6.   In Exhibit 1, an increase in demand would cause a move from which equilibrium point to another, other things being equal?

    a. E_1 to E_2.
    b. E_1 to E_3.
    c. E_4 to E_1.
    d. E_1 to E_4.

7.   In Exhibit 1, an increase in quantity supplied would cause a move from which equilibrium point to another, other things being equal?

    a. E_1 to E_2.
    b. E_1 to E_4.
    c. E_4 to E_1.
    d. E_3 to E_4.

8.   Beginning from an equilibrium at point E_2 in Exhibit 1, an increase in demand for good X, other things being equal, would move the equilibrium point to:

    a. E_1, no change.
    b. E_2.
    c. E_3.
    d. E_4.

9.   Suppose a price ceiling is set by the government below the market equilibrium price. Which of the following will result?

    a.   The demand curve will shift to the left.
    b.   The quantity demanded will exceed the quantity supplied.
    c.   The quantity supplied will exceed the quantity demanded.
    d.   There will be a surplus.

10.   Suppose a price floor is set by the government above the market equilibrium price. Which of the following will result?

    a.   There will be a surplus.
    b.   The quantity demanded will exceed the quantity supplied.
    c.   The demand curve will shift to the left.
    d.   None of the above.

11.   Suppose the government imposes rent control (a price ceiling) below the equilibrium price for rental housing. Which of the following will result?

a.   Black markets.
b.   The quality of existing rental housing deteriorates.
c.   Shortages.
d.   All of the above.

12.   If the equilibrium price of good X is $5 and a price ceiling is imposed at $4, the eventual result will be a (an):

a.   accumulation of inventories of unsold gas.
b.   shortage.
c.   surplus.
d.   all of the above.

13.   The former Soviet Union was known for black markets. An explanation for the existence of the black market is that:

a.   goods were not subject to price controls.
b.   the government imposed a price floor below the equilibrium price.
c.   the government imposed a price ceiling below the equilibrium price.
d.   all of the above.

Exhibit 2 Data on supply and demand

Bushels Demanded per month	Price per Bushel	Bushels Supplied per Month
45	$5	77
50	4	73
56	3	68
61	2	61
67	1	57

14.   In Exhibit 2, the equilibrium price per bushel of wheat is:

a. $1.
b. $2.
c. $3.
d. $4.

15.   Which of the following would occur if the government imposed a price floor (support price) of $4 per bushel in the wheat market shown in Exhibit 2?

a.   Buyers would want to purchase more wheat than is supplied.
b.   Buyers would not purchase all of the wheat grown.
c.   Shortage of wheat would increase the price of wheat.
d.   Farmers would grow less wheat.

16.   Which of the following is an example of market failure?

a.   Public goods.
b.   Externalities.
c.   Lack of competition.
d.   All of the above.

17.   A good that provides external benefits to society has:

a.   too few resources devoted to its production.
b.   too many resources devoted to its production.
c.   the optimal resources devoted to its production.
d.   not provided profits to producers of the good.

18.   Which of the following is a property of a public good?

a.   A public good is free from externalities.
b.   Many individuals benefit simultaneously.
c.   A public good is not subject to free riders.
d.   A public good is established by law.

19.   Which of the following is a public good?

a.   Air traffic control.
b.   National defense.
c.   Clean air.
d.   All of the above.

20.   Price ceilings are imposed if the government believes:

a.   the market will not achieve an equilibrium price.
b.   the market equilibrium price is too low.
c.   an excess supply of the product exists.
d.   the market equilibrium price is too high.
e.   the quantity demanded will less than the quantity supplied of the product.

21.   A third party is:

    a.   the party to which a contractual agreement is meant to benefit.
    b.   a person, or persons, who are unintentionally affected by the actions of others.
    c.   the third person in a three-way contract.
    d.   the person who owns the property right in a contract.
    e.   when the government attempts to mediate a dispute between management and labor.

22.   The city of Logan Square needs $40 million for a network of streetlights. There are 20,000 residents in the Logan Square neighborhood, meaning the cost for each resident is $2,000. Psychiatrist Denise Miller refuses to donate $2,000 towards the project. This is an example of the problems encountered with:

    a.   consumer goods.
    b.   capital goods.
    c.   rival goods.
    d.   public goods.
    e.   private goods.

■ TRUE OR FALSE

1.   T   F   In a market without government interference, the price is free to move the equilibrium.

2.   T   F   An equilibrium price is unaffected by nonprice factors.

3.   T   F   If the demand curve increases while the supply curve remains unchanged, the equilibrium price would decrease.

4.   T   F   If the supply curve decreases while the demand curve remains unchanged, the equilibrium price would decrease.

5.   T   F   Assume a ceiling price is set above the equilibrium price. The result is a shortage.

6.   T   F   Assume a price floor is set above the equilibrium price. The result is a surplus.

7.   T   F   A public good is any good or service that users collectively consume and there is no way to bar free riders.

8.   T   F   It's difficult for a private firm to provide a public good because of free riders.

■ CROSSWORD PUZZLE

Fill in the crossword puzzle from the list of key concepts. Not all of the concepts are used.

ACROSS

7.   Vaccinations.

DOWN

1.   A maximum price set by the government.
2.   Pollution.
3.   A situation in which the price system creates
      a problem for society or fails to achieve society's goals.
4.   A cost or benefit imposed on people.
5.   A minimum price set by the government.
6.   A good with a free rider problem.

■ ANSWERS

Completion Questions

1. price ceiling
2. price floor
3. external cost
4. external benefits
5. public good
6. market failure
7. externality

Multiple Choice

1. a 2. b 3. d 4. c 5. c 6. d 7. b 8. c 9. b 10. a 11. d 12. b 13. c 14. b 15. b 16. d
17. a 18. b 19. d 20. d 21. b 22. d

True or False

1. True 2. False 3. False 4. False 5. False 6. True 7. True 8. True

Crossword Puzzle

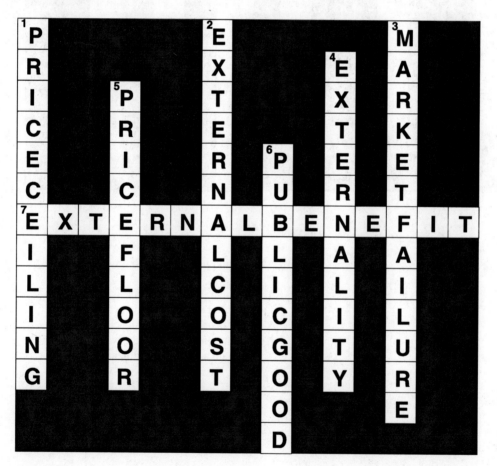

Chapter 5
Price Elasticity of Demand

■ CHAPTER IN A NUTSHELL

This chapter introduces the concept of price elasticity of demand. Elasticity can be thought of as "sensitivity." The price elasticity of demand measures how sensitive the quantity demanded is to a change in price. Based on the calculation of an elasticity coefficient, demand can be classified as: elastic, inelastic, unitary elastic, perfectly elastic, or perfectly inelastic. Applications in the chapter demonstrate the relationship between price elasticity of demand and changes in total revenue in response to price changes. For example, if the price increases along an elastic segment of a demand curve, total revenue decreases. The chapter concludes with a discussion of determinants of price elasticity of demand. These factors include: availability of substitutes, share of budget, and adjustment to price over time.

■ KEY CONCEPTS

Elastic demand	Price elasticity of demand
Inelastic demand	Total revenue
Perfectly elastic demand	Unitary elastic demand
Perfectly inelastic demand	

■ LEARNING OBJECTIVES

After completing this chapter, you should be able to:

1. Understand that price elasticity of demand is a measure of consumer responsiveness with respect to the amount purchased given a price change.
2. Calculate and interpret an elastic, inelastic, unitary elastic, perfectly elastic and perfectly inelastic demand using the mid-points formula and the total revenue test.
3. Determine those factors which contribute to an inelastic and elastic demand for a product.
4. Explain why the price elasticity of demand varies along a given demand curve.
5. Illustrate perfectly elastic and inelastic demand curves graphically.

■ COMPLETION QUESTIONS

1. The ratio of the percentage change in quantity demanded to the percentage change in price is called _____.

2. _____ is a more than 1 percent change in quantity demanded in response to a 1 percent change in price.

3. _____ is a less than 1 percent change in quantity demanded in response to a 1 percent change in price.

4. _____ is a 1 percent change in quantity demanded in response to a 1 percent change in price.

5. An extreme case in which the demand curve is horizontal and the elasticity coefficient equals infinity is called _____.

6. An extreme case in which the demand curve is vertical and the elasticity coefficient equals zero is called _____.

7. The total number of dollars a firm earns from the sale of a good or service, which is equal to its price multiplied by the quantity demanded is called _____.

■ MULTIPLE CHOICE

1. If a decrease in the price of football tickets increases the total revenue of the athletic department, this is evidence that demand is:

    a. price elastic.
    b. price inelastic.
    c. unit elastic with respect to price.
    d. perfectly inelastic.

2. If the percentage change in the quantity demanded of a good is greater than the percentage change in price, price elasticity of demand is:

    a. elastic.
    b. inelastic.
    c. perfectly inelastic.
    d. perfectly elastic.

3. Suppose the president of a textbook publisher argues that a 10 percent increase in the price of textbooks will raise total revenue for the publisher. It can be concluded that the company president thinks that demand for textbooks is:

    a. unitary elastic.
    b. inelastic.
    c. elastic.
    d. perfectly inelastic.

4. If the quantity of tickets to the fair sold decreases by 10 percent when the price increases by 5 percent, the price elasticity of demand over this range of the demand curve is:

    a. price elastic.
    b. price inelastic.
    c. perfectly inelastic.
    d. unitary elastic.

5.   There is no change in total revenue when the demand curve for a good is:

    a.   unitary elastic.
    b.   perfectly inelastic.
    c.   elastic.
    d.   inelastic.
    e.   perfectly elastic.

6.   Which of the following is *true* for a lower price elasticity of demand coefficient?

    a.   The quantity demanded is less responsive.
    b.   Few substitutes exist.
    c.   Many substitutes exist.
    d.   All of the above.

7.   Elasticity refers to the:

    a.   percentage increase in price in response to a percentage increase in quantity demanded.
    b.   percentage decrease in price in response to a percentage increase in income.
    c.   minimum amount that consumers will pay for a percentage change in quantity demanded or supplied.
    d.   responsiveness of quantity demanded to changes in the price of a good.

8.   Along a straight-line, downward-sloping demand curve,

    a.   price elasticity of demand remains constant.
    b.   price elasticity of demand equals the slope of the line.
    c.   price elasticity of demand varies along the curve.
    d.   total revenue remains constant.

9.   You are on a campus committee which sets the ticket prices for basketball games. The committee wants to increase the total money generated from ticket sales. When should the committee choose to lower its ticket prices?

    a.   Always.
    b.   Never.
    c.   When demand for basketball tickets is elastic.
    d.   When demand for basketball tickets is inelastic.

10.   A 10 percent rise in the price of housing reduces the quantity demanded of housing by 3 percent. We can conclude that the demand for housing is:

    a.   inelastic.
    b.   elastic.
    c.   unitary elastic.
    d.   perfectly elastic.

11.   If a decrease in the price of movie tickets increases the total revenue of movie theaters, this is evidence that demand is:

    a.   price elastic.
    b.   price inelastic.
    c.   unit elastic.
    d.   perfectly inelastic.

12.   Suppose the president of a college argues that a 25 percent tuition increase will raise revenues for the college. It can be concluded that the president thinks that demand to attend this college is:

    a.   elastic, but not perfectly elastic.
    b.   inelastic, but not perfectly inelastic.
    c.   unitary elastic.
    d.   coefficient effective.

13.   Suppose an oil company wants to make its total revenue as large as possible. It should charge a price at which the demand for oil is:

    a.   elastic.
    b.   unitary elastic.
    c.   inelastic.
    d.   perfectly inelastic.

14.   The president of Tucker Motors says, "Lowering the price won't sell a single additional Tucker car." The president believes that the price elasticity of a demand is:

    a.   perfectly elastic.
    b.   perfectly inelastic.
    c.   unitary elastic.
    d.   elastic.
    e.   inelastic.

15.   If demand is price elastic, a decrease in price causes:

    a.   an increase in total revenue.
    b.   a decrease in total revenue.
    c.   no change in total revenue.
    d.   an increase in quantity, but anything can happen to revenue.

16.   Leo's Bakery reduces the price of wheat bread from $3 to $1 and finds that quantity demanded increases from 100 to 120 loaves. Leo calculates that his price elasticity of demand for wheat bread is:

a.   0.
b.   0.18.
c.   1.0.
d.   1.5.
e.   2.

17.   Tara buys four music cassettes when the price is $10 and two cassettes when the price is $14. Her price elasticity of demand is:

a.   0.
b.   1.
c.   2.
d.   3.
e.   4.

Exhibit 1 Demand curves

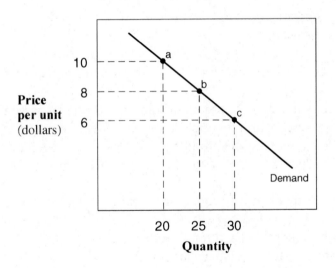

18.   In Exhibit 1, between points a and b, the price elasticity of demand measures:

a.   .67.
b.   1.5.
c.   2.0.
d.   1.56.
e.   1.0.

19.   In Exhibit 1, between points b and c, the price elasticity of demand measures:

a.   4.27.
b.   1.5.
c.   1.56.
d.   .636.
e.   .425.

20.   In Exhibit 1, the demand curve between points a and b is:

a.   price elastic.
b.   price inelastic.
c.   unit elastic.
d.   perfectly elastic.
e.   perfectly inelastic.

21.   In Exhibit 1, the demand curve between points b and c is:

a.   price elastic.
b.   price inelastic.
c.   unit elastic.
d.   perfectly elastic.
e.   perfectly inelastic.

22.   If demand price elasticity measures 2, this implies that consumers would:

a.   buy twice as much of the product if the price drops 10 percent.
b.   require a 2 percent drop in price to increase their purchases by 1 percent.
c.   buy 2 percent more of the product in response to a 1 percent drop in price.
d.   require at least a $2 increase in price before showing any response to the price increase.
e.   buy twice as much of the product if the price drops 1 percent.

23.   If the price elasticity of demand for a product measures .45,
a.   this good has many available substitutes.
b.   this good must be a nonessential good.
c.   this good is a high-priced good.
d.   a decrease in price will increase total revenue.
e.   this good is demand price inelastic.

24.   Suppose the quantity of steak purchased by the Jones family is 110 pounds per year when the price is $2.10 per pound and 90 pounds per year when the price is $3.90 per pound. The price elasticity of demand coefficient for this family is:

a.   0.33.
b.   0.50.
c.   1.00.
d.   2.00.

■ TRUE OR FALSE

1.   T   F   If a 10 percent price increase causes the quantity demanded for a good to decrease by 20 percent, demand is elastic.

2.   T   F   If a 10 percent price increase causes the quantity demanded for a good to decrease by 5 percent, demand is elastic.

3.   T   F   If a 10 percent price increase causes the quantity demanded for a good to decrease by 10 percent, demand is unitary elastic.

4.   T   F   If the demand curve for a good is elastic, consumers will spend more on that good when its price increases.

5.   T   F   Suppose an economist found that total revenues increased for the bus system when fares were raised. The conclusion is that the price elasticity demand for subway services over the range of fare increase is inelastic.

6.   T   F   A horizontal demand curve is perfectly elastic.

7.   T   F   If a good has a price elasticity of demand coefficient greater than 1, total revenue can be increased by raising the price.

8.   T   F   Other factors held constant, if there are few close substitutes for a good, demand is more elastic for it.

9.   T   F   If a good has a price elasticity of demand coefficient greater than 1, total revenue can be increased by raising the price.

10.   T   F   If the demand for a product is inelastic, then a price increase will result in a decrease in total revenue.

■ CROSSWORD PUZZLE

Fill in the crossword puzzle from the list of key concepts. Not all of the concepts are used.

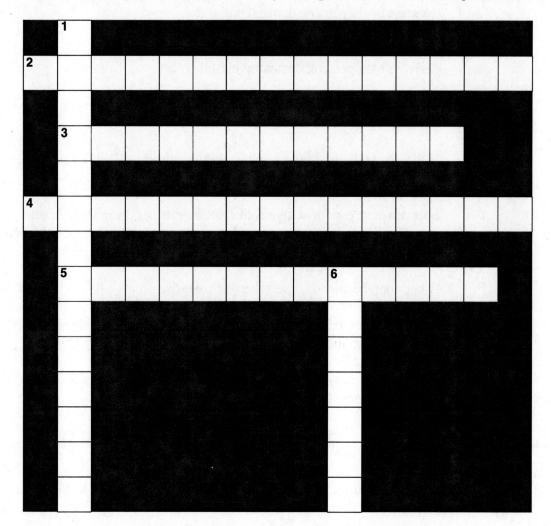

ACROSS

2.   The percentage change in quantity demanded is less than the percentage change in price.
3.   The price multiplied by the quantity demanded.
4.   The percentage change in quantity demanded divided by the percentage change in price.
5.   The percentage change in quantity demanded exceeds the percentage change in price.

DOWN

1.   The percentage change in price causes an equal percentage change in quantity demanded.
6.   A perfectly _____ demand is a condition in which a small percentage change in price brings about an infinite percentage change in quantity demanded.

 **ANSWERS**

Completion Questions

1. price elasticity of demand
2. elastic demand
3. inelastic demand
4. unitary elastic demand
5. perfectly elastic demand
6. perfectly inelastic demand
7. total revenue

Multiple Choice

1. a. 2. a 3. b 4. a 5. a 6. a 7. d 8. c 9.c 10.a 11. a 12. b 13. b 14. b 15. a 16. b 17. c
18. e 19. d 20. c 21. b 22. c 23. e 24. a

True or False

1. True 2. False 3. True 4. False 5. True 6. True 7. False 8. False 9. False 10. False

Crossword Puzzle

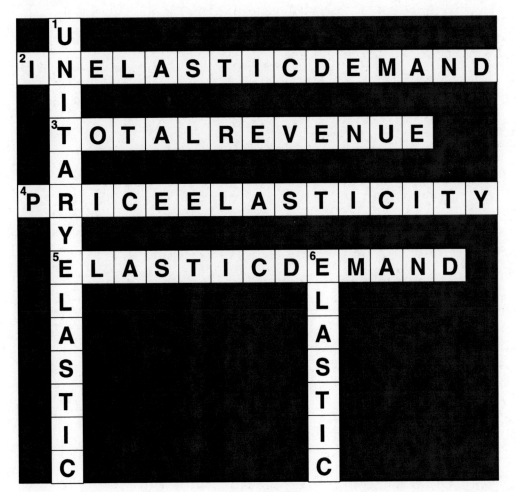

Chapter 6
Production Costs

■ CHAPTER IN A NUTSHELL

The main objective of this chapter is to introduce the different cost concepts that will be applied in later chapters. You begin by learning about the production function, which shows the maximum output that can be produced from various quantities of inputs. The law of diminishing returns states that, beyond some point, the marginal product of a variable input will diminish in the short run. In the short run, three kinds of cost curves are important: total cost, total fixed cost, and total variable cost. Corresponding to each of the total cost curves are three average cost curves: average total cost, average fixed cost, and average variable cost. Marginal cost is the addition to total cost due to the production of an additional unit of output. The chapter concludes with a discussion of the firm's long-run cost curve, which is the relationship between various possible plant sizes and the minimum average cost of production.

■ KEY CONCEPTS

Average fixed cost
Average variable cost
Average total cost
Constant returns to scale
Diseconomies of scale
Economic profit
Economies of scale
Explicit costs
Fixed input
Implicit costs
Law of diminishing returns

Long run
Long-run average cost curve
Marginal cost
Marginal product
Normal profit
Production function
Short run
Total fixed cost
Total variable cost
Total cost
Variable input

■ LEARNING OBJECTIVES

After completing this chapter, you should be able to:

1. Distinguish between explicit and implicit cost.
2. Distinguish between economic and accounting profit, and explain why economists are interested in economic profit and not accounting profit.
3. Explain the difference between the short-run and the long-run.
4. Define the law of diminishing returns, and explain the relationship between inputs and output in the context of a production function.
5. Define all seven short-run cost figures, express them graphically, calculate them numerically and graphically, and understand the relationship between them.
6. Define what is meant by economies, constant, and diseconomies of scale, understand why they exist, and express them graphically.

THE ECONOMIST'S TOOL KIT
Graphing Cost Curves

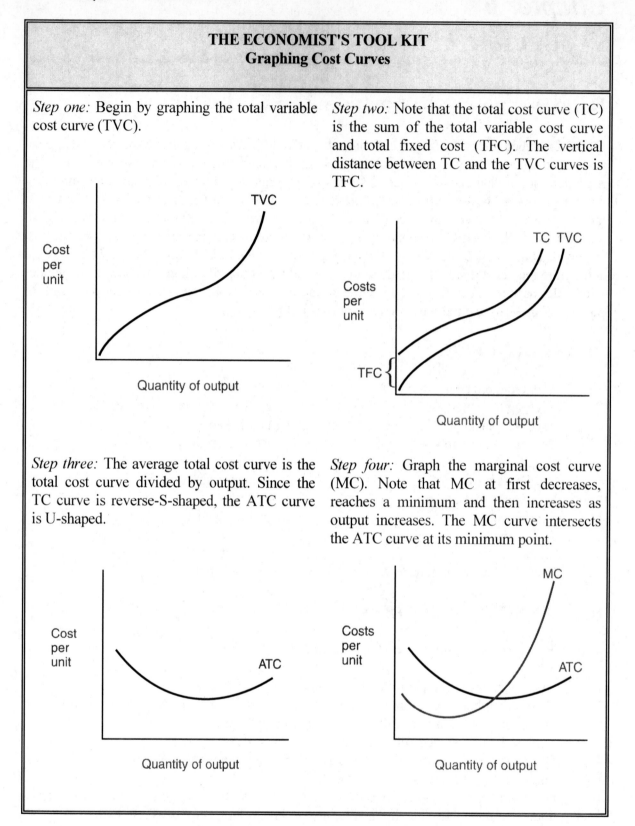

Step one: Begin by graphing the total variable cost curve (TVC).

Step two: Note that the total cost curve (TC) is the sum of the total variable cost curve and total fixed cost (TFC). The vertical distance between TC and the TVC curves is TFC.

Step three: The average total cost curve is the total cost curve divided by output. Since the TC curve is reverse-S-shaped, the ATC curve is U-shaped.

Step four: Graph the marginal cost curve (MC). Note that MC at first decreases, reaches a minimum and then increases as output increases. The MC curve intersects the ATC curve at its minimum point.

■ COMPLETION QUESTIONS

1. _____ is equal to total revenue minus both explicit and implicit costs.

2. The opportunity cost of resources owned by the firm are called _____ .

3. The _____ is a time period during which a firm cannot alter some input such as its factory size.

4. A (an) _____ is the relationship between output and inputs.

5. After some level of output in the short run, each unit of the variable input yields smaller and smaller marginal product. This principle is called the _____ .

6. _____ includes costs, such as rent for office space, that cannot vary with the level of output.

7. _____, such as wages, vary as the level of output varies.

8. _____ is the change in total cost associated with a change in one unit of output.

9. _____ is the sum of average fixed cost and average variable cost.

10. When long-run average cost decreases as output increases, the firm experiences _____ .

11. Payments to nonowners of a firm for their resources are called _____

12. _____ is the minimum profit necessary to keep a firm in operation.

13. Any resource for which the quantity cannot change during the period of time under consideration is called _____ .

14. A period of time so long that all inputs are variable is called a (an) _____ .

15. _____ is the change in total output produced by adding one unit of a variable input, with all other inputs used being held constant.

16. Any resource for which the quantity can change during the period of time under consideration is called _____ .

17.   The sum of total fixed cost and total variable cost at each level of output is called

_____.

18.   _____ is the total fixed cost divided by the quantity of output produced.

19.   Total variable cost divided by the quantity of output produced is called

_____.

20.   The rule that states when marginal cost is below average cost, average cost falls. When marginal cost is above average cost, average cost rises. When marginal cost equals average cost, average cost is at its minimum point is called the_____.

21.   The _____ traces the lowest cost per unit at which a firm can produce any level of output when the firm can build any desired plant size.

22.   _____ is a situation in which the long-run average cost curve does not change as the firm increases output.

23.   A situation in which the long-run average cost curve rises as the firm increases output is called _____.

◼ MULTIPLE CHOICE

1.   Payments to nonowners of a firm are called:

a.   implicit costs.
b.   indirect costs.
c.   explicit costs.
d.   economic costs.

2.   An economist left his $100,000-a-year teaching position to work full-time in his own consulting business. In the first year, he had total revenue of $200,000 and business expenses of $150,000. He made a (an):

a.   implicit profit.
b.   economic loss.
c.   economic profit.
d.   accounting loss but not an economic loss.
e.   zero economic profit.

3.   Normal profit is defined as a (an):

a.   implicit profit.
b.   opportunity profit.
c.   the minimum profit necessary to keep a firm in business.
d.   all of the above.

4.   A farm is able to produce 5,000 bushels of peaches per season on 100 acres. Assume it adds one more acre and is able to produce 6,000 bushels per season. The marginal product of the additional acre of land for this farm is:

a.   6,000 bushels per acre per year.
b.   5,000 bushels per acre per year.
c.   1,000 bushels per acre per year.
d.   11,000 bushels per acre per year.

5.   The _____ is the situation in which the marginal product of labor is greater than zero and declining as more labor is hired.

a.   law of demand.
b.   law of diminishing supply.
c.   law of diminishing returns.
d.   law of returns to scale.

Exhibit 1 Cost schedule for Firm X

Output Quantity	Total Fixed Cost	Total Variable Cost
0	$100	$ 0
1	100	50
2	100	84
3	100	108
4	100	127
5	100	150

6.   As shown in Exhibit 1, the marginal cost of producing the fifth unit is:

a. $23.
b. $16.
c. $24.
d. $50.

7.   As shown in Exhibit 1, the total cost of producing 5 units is:

a. $100.
b. $227.
c. $250.
d.   zero.

8. As shown in Exhibit 1, the total cost of producing 3 units is:

    a. $100.
    b. $227.
    c. $208.
    d. zero.

Exhibit 2 Long-run average cost

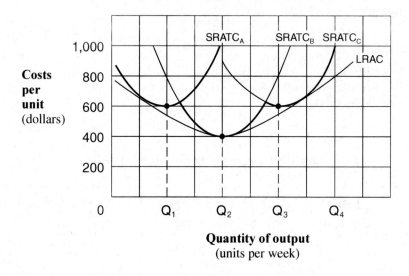

Quantity of output
(units per week)

9. Given the short-run average total cost curves in Exhibit 2, what level of output per week minimizes average total cost?

    a. Q_1 units.
    b. Q_2 units.
    c. Q_3 units.
    d. Q_4 units.

10. In Exhibit 2, economies of scale exist up to:

    a. Q_1 units of output per week.
    b. Q_2 units of output per week.
    c. Q_3 units of output.
    d. Q_4 units of output.

11. In Exhibit 2, short-run average total cost, short-run marginal cost, and long-run average cost are all equal at which level of output per week?

    a. Q_1 units.
    b. Q_2 units.
    c. Q_3 units.
    d. Q_4 units.

12.   If the firm represented in Exhibit 2 is operating with a plant whose size corresponds to short-run average total cost curve A, the level of output that would minimize its short-run average total cost is:

    a. Q_1 units per week.
    b. Q_2 units per week.
    c. Q_3 units per week.
    d. Q_4 units per week.

13.   If the units of variable input in a production process are 1, 2, 3, 4, and 5, and the corresponding total outputs are 30, 34, 37, 39, and 40, respectively. The marginal product of the fourth unit is:

    a.   2.
    b.   1.
    c.   37.
    d.   39.

14.   Which of the following is *true* at the point where diminishing returns set in?

    a.   Both marginal product and marginal cost are at a maximum.
    b.   Both marginal product and marginal cost are at a minimum.
    c.   Marginal product is at a maximum and marginal cost at a minimum.
    d.   Marginal product is at a minimum and marginal cost at a maximum.

15.   Assume both the marginal cost and the average variable cost curves are U-shaped. At the minimum point on the average variable cost curve, marginal cost must be:

    a.   greater than average variable cost.
    b.   less than average variable cost.
    c.   equal to average variable cost.
    d.   at its minimum.

16.   Which of the following statements is *true*?

    a.   Economic profit equals accounting profit minus implicit costs.
    b.   The short run is any period of time in which there is at least one fixed input.
    c.   A fixed input is any resource for which the quantity cannot change during the period under consideration.
    d.   In the long run there are no fixed costs.
    e.   All of the above.

17.   Which of the following statements is *true?*

a.   The law of diminishing returns states that beyond some point the marginal product of a variable resource continues to rise.
b.   The marginal product is the change in total output by adding one additional unit of a fixed input.
c.   Fixed costs are costs which vary with the output level.
d.   When marginal productivity of a variable input is falling then marginal costs of production must be rising.
e.   When marginal cost is below average cost, average cost rises; when marginal cost is above average cost, average cost falls.

18.   Which of the following statements is *false?*

a.   TC = TFC + TVC.
b.   AVC = ATC – AFC.
c.   AFC = TFC/Q.
d.   MC equals the change in ATC divided by the change in Q.
e.   ATC = TC/Q.

19.   If a firm enlarges its factory size and realizes higher average (per unit) costs of production then:

a.   it has experienced economies of scale.
b.   it has experienced diseconomies of scale.
c.   it has experienced constant returns to scale.
d.   the long-run average cost curve slopes downward.
e.   the long-run average cost curve shifts upward.

20.   The lowest point on the average total cost curve is:

a.   where it intersects the marginal cost curve.
b.   where it intersects the average variable cost curve.
c.   where it intersects the average fixed cost curve.
d.   where marginal product is maximized.

21.   Which of the following *best* describes a production function?

a.   The relationship between consumer preferences and market demand.
b.   The relationship between the quantity of labor employed and total cost.
c.   The relationship between the maximum amounts of output a firm can produce and various quantities of inputs.
d.   The relationship between price and quantity supplied by sellers in a market.

■ TRUE OR FALSE

1.   T   F   Suppose Joe Rich owns his own company and does not pay himself a salary. This means the salary he could have earned in alternative employment is considered an implicit cost for the firm.

2.   T   F   Suppose a firm earns an accounting profit. This means the firm also earns a positive economic profit.

3.   T   F   In the short-run, total fixed costs always exceed total variable costs.

4.   T   F   A firm's marginal product of labor curve slopes downward throughout its length.

5.   T   F   In the long run, all costs are considered variable.

6.   T   F   Marginal cost is calculated by dividing the change in total cost by the change in total output.

7.   T   F   If the total variable cost of producing 5 units of output is $10 and the total variable cost of producing 6 units is $15, the marginal cost of producing a sixth unit is $5.

8.   T   F   All of a firm's inputs are considered to be variable in the long run.

9.   T   F   Each short-run average total cost curve is tangent at its lowest point to the long-run average cost curve.

10.   T   F   Economies of scale exist over all ranges of output for which short-run average total cost exceeds long-run average cost.

■ CROSSWORD PUZZLE

Fill in the crossword puzzle from the list of key concepts. Not all of the concepts are used.

ACROSS

2.   The law of _____ returns is the principle that beyond some point the marginal product decreases as additional units of a variable factor are added to a fixed factor.

4.   The average _____ cost is the total variable cost divided by the quantity of output produced.

6.   A resource for which the quantity cannot change.

7.   The sum of total fixed cost and total variable cost.

10.   _____ costs are opportunity costs of using resources owned by the firm.

11.   Marginal_____ is the change in total output produced by adding one unit of a variable input, with all other inputs used being held constant.

12.   The average _____ cost is the total cost divided by the quantity of output produced.

DOWN

1.   Economic _____ is the total revenue minus explicit and implicit costs.

3.   The change in total cost when one unit is produced.

5.   _____ costs are payments to nonowners of a firm for their resources.

8.   A period of time in which at least one input is fixed.

9.   The average _____ cost is the total fixed cost divided by the quantity of output produced.

Completion Questions

1. economic profit
2. implicit costs
3. short run
4. production function
5. law of diminishing returns
6. total fixed cost
7. total variable cost
8. marginal cost
9. average total cost
10. economies of scale
11. explicit costs
12. normal profit
13. fixed input
14. long run
15. marginal product
16. variable input
17. total costs
18. average fixed costs
19. average variable cost
20. marginal-average rule
21. long-run average cost curve
22. constant returns to scale
23. diseconomies of scale

Multiple Choice

1. c 2. b. 3. c 4. c 5. c 6. a 7. c 8. c. 9. b 10. b 11. b 12. a 13. a 14. c 15. c 16. e 17. d 18. d 19. b 20. a 21. c

True or False

1. True 2. False 3. False 4. False 5. True 6. True 7. True 8. True 9. False
10. False

Crossword Puzzle

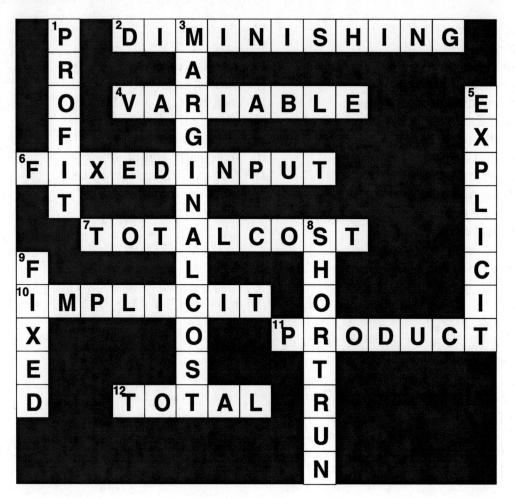

Chapter 7
Perfect Competition

■ CHAPTER IN A NUTSHELL

This chapter develops the perfectly competitive market structure. Perfect competition requires a large number of firms, firms producing a homogeneous product, and very easy entry into or exit from the market. Given these characteristics, the perfectly competitive firm faces a horizontal demand curve and is a "price taker." Using marginal analysis, the firm will maximize profits, or minimize losses, by producing a level of output in the short run where marginal cost equals marginal revenue (price). However, if the price is below average variable cost, the firm shuts down. From these basic rules it follows that the firm's supply curve is its marginal cost curve for prices above average variable curve. In the long run, equilibrium is achieved through the entry and exit of firms until economic profit equals zero.

■ KEY CONCEPTS

Marginal revenue
Market structure
Perfect competition
Perfectly competitive firm's short-run supply curve
Perfectly competitive industry's short-run supply curve
Price taker

■ LEARNING OBJECTIVES

After completing this chapter, you should be able to:

1. Describe the characteristics of competitive market environments.
2. Graphically express the competitive firm's demand curve and understand that this curve reflects the fact that the competitive firm is a price taker.
3. Graphically find the profit maximizing quantity to produce and explain why this output is the profit maximizing quantity.
4. Graphically determine the area representing any economic profits or losses.
5. Find on a graph the competitive firm's short-run supply curve and explain in words why this is the case.
6. Derive the industry's short-run supply curve.
7. Explain what is expected to happen over time given short-run economic profits or losses and express this graphically.
8. Graphically illustrate long-run equilibrium for a competitive industry and explain why this is the case.

■ COMPLETION QUESTIONS

1. _____ consists of three market characteristics: (1) the number of sellers, (2) nature of the product, and (3) the ease or exit from the market.

2. Under_____ the firm is very small relative to the market as a whole, sells a homogeneous product, and firms in the industry are free to enter and exit.

3. A firm in perfect competition is a (an) _____ because it can sell all it wishes at the market determined price, but it will sell nothing above the given market price.

4. A change in total revenue from a one unit change in output is called _____

5. The _____ for a perfectly competitive firm is a curve showing the relationship between the price of a product and the quantity supplied in the short run. The individual firm always produces along its marginal cost curve above its intersection with the average variable cost curve.

6. The _____ for a perfectly competitive firm is the horizontal summation of all firm's short-run supply curves in the industry.

7. The _____ is a curve that shows the quantities supplied by the industry at different prices after firms complete their entry and exit.

■ MULTIPLE CHOICE

1. Market structure describes which of the following characteristics?

    a.   The ease of entry into and exit from the market.
    b.   The similarity of the product sold.
    c.   The number of firms in each industry.
    d.   All of the above are true.

2. Under perfect competition, a firm is a price taker because:

    a.   setting a price higher than the going price results in profits.
    b.   each firm's product is perceived as different.
    c.   each firm has a significant market share.
    d.   setting a price higher than the going price results in zero sales.

3.   In the short run, a perfectly competitive firm's *most* profitable level of output is where:

   a.   marginal cost exceeds marginal revenue.
   b.   total revenue is at a maximum.
   c.   marginal cost equals marginal revenue.
   d.   All of the above.

Exhibit 1 Marginal revenue and cost per unit curves

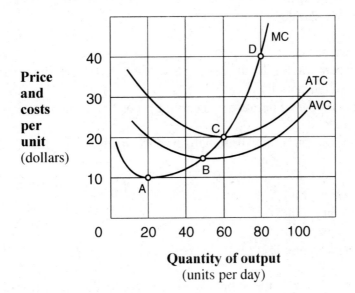

4.   As shown in Exhibit 1, if the product is either $10, $15, $20, or $40 the firm's economic profit is maximum at an output of:

   a.   20 units per day.
   b.   40 units per day.
   c.   60 units per day.
   d.   80 units per day.

5.   In Exhibit 1, if the price of the firm's product is $20 per unit, the firm will produce:

   a.   20 units per day.
   b.   40 units per day.
   c.   60 units per day.
   d.   80 units per day.

6. As shown in Exhibit 1, the price at which the firm earns zero economic profit in the short-run is:

 a. $10 per unit.
 b. $15 per unit.
 c. $40 per unit.
 d. more than $20 per unit.
 e. $20 per unit.

7. If the price of the firm's product in Exhibit 1 is $15 per unit, which intersects AVC at point B, the firm should:

 a. shut down permanently.
 b. stay in operation for the time being even though it is making a pure economic loss.
 c. shut down temporarily.
 d. continue to operate because it is earning a positive economic profit.

8. As shown in Exhibit 1, the firm will produce in the short run if the price is at least equal to:

 a. $10 per unit (point A).
 b. $15 per unit (point B).
 c. $20 per unit (point C).
 d. $40 per unit (point D).

9. As shown in Exhibit 1, the short-run supply curve for the firm corresponds to which segment of its marginal cost curve?

 a. C and all points above.
 b. B and all points above.
 c. A and all points above.
 d. A to C only.
 e. B to D only.

10. In long-run equilibrium, the typical perfectly competitive firm will:

 a. earn zero economic profit.
 b. change plant size in the long run.
 c. change output in the short run.
 d. do any of the above.

11. In long-run equilibrium for a perfectly competitive firm, price equals which of the following?

 a. Economies of real cost.
 b. Maximum total revenue.
 c. Diseconomies of scale cost.
 d. Minimum point on the long-run average cost curve.

12.   In a perfectly competitive industry, assume there is a permanent increase in demand for a product. The process of transition to a new long-run equilibrium will include:

   a.   the exit of firms.
   b.   temporarily lower production costs.
   c.   both a and b.
   d.   neither a nor b.

13.   In a perfectly competitive industry, assume the short-run average total cost increases as the output of the industry expands. In the long run, the industry supply curve will:

   a.   first have a positive slope and then a negative slope.
   b.   have a negative slope.
   c.   be perfectly horizontal.
   d.   be perfectly vertical.
   e.   have a positive slope.

14.   Assume that a firm's marginal revenue just barely exceeds marginal cost. Under these conditions the firm should:

   a.   expand output.
   b.   contract output.
   c.   maintain output.
   d.   There is insufficient information to answer the question.

15.   Perfectly competitive markets are characterized by:

   a.   a small number of very large producers.
   b.   very strong barriers to entry and exit.
   c.   firms selling a homogeneous product.
   d.   all of the above.

16.   Which of the following is *true* of a perfectly competitive firm?

   a.   The firm is a price maker.
   b.   If the firm wishes to maximize profits it will produce an output level in which total revenue equals total cost.
   c.   The firm will not earn an economic profit in the long run.
   d.   The firm's short-run supply curve is its MC curve below its AVC curve.

17.   The profit maximizing, or loss minimizing, quantity of output for any firm to produce exists at that output level in which:

   a.   total revenue is maximized.
   b.   total cost is minimized.
   c.   marginal cost is minimized.
   d.   marginal revenue equals marginal cost.

18.   If a competitive firm is incurring economic losses, then it should:

    a.   always shut down.
    b.   shut down if losses are greater than total fixed costs.
    c.   shut down if total fixed costs are greater than losses.
    d.   raise its price.

19.   Which of the following is *true* of a perfectly competitive market?

    a.   If economic profits are earned then the price will fall over time.
    b.   In long-run equilibrium $P = MR = SRMC = SRATC = LRAC$.
    c.   Economic profits are zero in the long run.
    d.   All of the above.

20.   In long-run equilibrium, a competitive firm produces the level of output at which:
    a.   marginal cost is at a minimum.
    b.   short-run average total cost and long-run average cost are at a minimum.
    c.   total revenue is at a maximum.
    d.   diseconomies of scale end.

■ TRUE OR FALSE

1.   T   F   A perfectly competitive market is characterized by the free entry and exit of firms.

2.   T   F   A perfectly competitive market is characterized by highly advertised goods.

3.   T   F   If marginal revenue exceeds marginal cost in the short run, the perfectly competitive firm maximizes economic profit.

4.   T   F   If marginal revenue exceeds marginal cost in the short-run, total revenue for the perfectly competitive firm is greater than total cost.

5.   T   F   A perfectly competitive firm will shut down in the short-run when marginal revenue equals marginal cost at a price less than minimum average variable cost.

6.   T   F   The short-run supply curve and short-run marginal cost curve for a perfectly competitive firm coincide when the market price is greater than average variable cost.

7.   T   F   A perfectly competitive firm shuts down in the short-run when the market price is less than the average variable cost.

8.   T   F   In long-run equilibrium, a perfectly competitive firm's short-run marginal cost curve crosses the long-run average cost curve at the lowest point on the long-run average cost curve.

9. T F In the long run, a competitive firm will earn zero economic profit.

10. T F When faced with an economic loss, a competitive firm will exit the industry in the long run.

■ CROSSWORD PUZZLE

Fill in the crossword puzzle from the list of key concepts. Not all of the concepts are used.

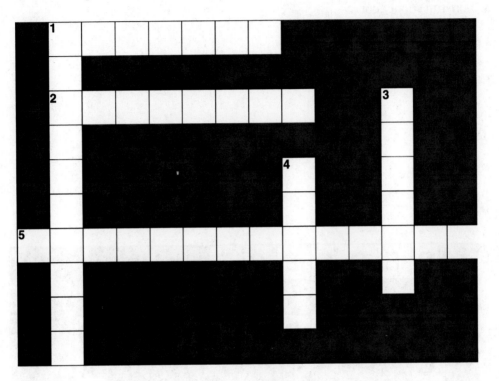

ACROSS

1. _____ competition is a market structure with a large number of small firms.
2. A perfectly competitive _____ short-run supply curve is derived from the horizontal summation of all firms' marginal cost curves in the industry above the minimum point of each firm's average variable cost curve.
5. The change in total revenue from the sale of one additional unit of output.

DOWN

1. Seller that has no control over price.
3. _____ structure is a classification system for key traits of a market.
4. A perfectly competitive _____ short-run supply curve is the firm's marginal cost curve above the minimum point on its average variable cost curve.

■ ANSWERS

Completion Questions

1. market structure
2. perfect competition
3. price taker
4. marginal revenue
5. firm's short-run supply curve

6. industry's short-run supply curve
7. industry's long-run supply curve

Multiple Choice

1. d 2. d 3. c 4. d 5. c 6. e 7. b 8. b 9. b 10. a 11. d 12. d 13. e 14. a 15. c 16. c 17. d 18. b 19. d 20. b

True or False

1. True 2. False 3. False 4. False 5. True 6. True 7. True 8. True 9. True 10. True

Crossword Puzzle

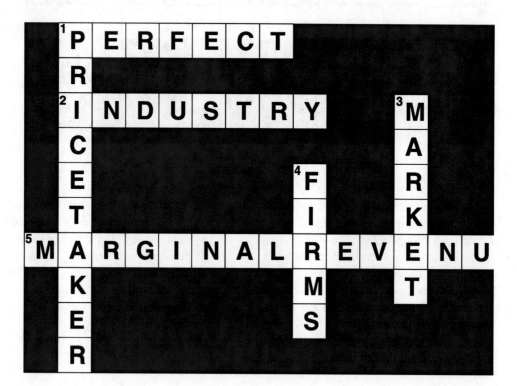

Chapter 8
Monopoly

■ CHAPTER IN A NUTSHELL

With the study of perfect competition complete in the previous chapter, this chapter explains how prices are set in monopolies. The source of monopoly market power is an impossible barrier to entry for potential competitors because of ownership of key resources, legal barriers, or economies of scale. Since the monopolist is the only seller of a product, the demand facing the monopolist is the entire market demand curve. As under perfect competition, the monopolist will maximize profit by choosing the output where marginal cost equals the marginal revenue. However, since the marginal revenue curve is below the demand curve, price does not equal marginal revenue for the monopolist as under perfect competition. The chapter concludes with a discussion of price discrimination and a comparison of monopoly and perfect competition. An important conclusion is that the output under perfect competition is greater and the price lower than under monopoly.

■ KEY CONCEPTS

Arbitrage
Monopoly
Natural monopoly
Network good
Price discrimination
Price maker

■ LEARNING OBJECTIVES

After completing this chapter, you should be able to:

1. Describe the characteristics of the monopoly market environment.
2. Graphically express the monopolist's demand curve and understand that this curve is really the market demand curve.
3. Graphically find the profit maximizing quantity to produce and explain why this output is the profit maximizing quantity.
4. Graphically determine the area representing any economic profits or losses.
5. Find on a graph the monopolist's short-run supply curve and explain why this is also the industry's short-run supply curve.
6. Explain why short-run economic profits may persist in the long run.
7. Explain what is meant by price discrimination, what must be accomplished in order to do so, and why a monopolist may price discriminate.
8. Compare and contrast the competitive market environment and the monopoly market.
9. List the monopoly disadvantages from society's perspective.

THE ECONOMIST'S TOOL KIT
Finding the Monopolist's Price and Output

Step one: Because the monopolist is the only seller in the industry, the monopolist can select any price along a downward-sloping demand curve.

Step two: Begin with the marginal revenue curve (MR) drawn from the point where the demand curve intersects the price axis. Connect the MR line to a point half the distance from where the demand curve intersects the quantity axis.

Step three: Here we include cost by drawing the marginal cost curve (MC) in the graph.

Step four: The monopolist's profit maximizing price and output level is determined were MC = MR.

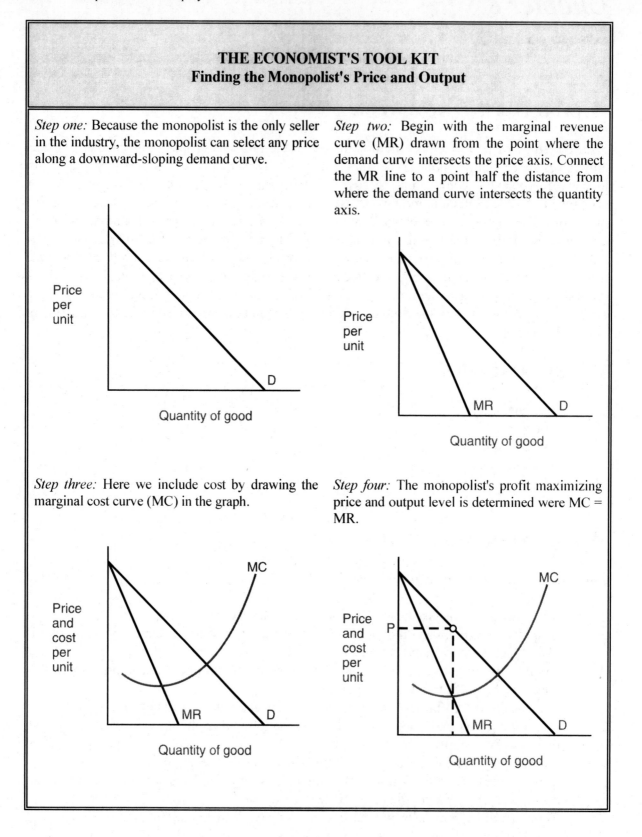

■ COMPLETION QUESTIONS

1. _____ is a single seller facing the entire industry demand curve. The reason for this type of market structure is that the firm sells a unique product and extremely high barriers to entry protect it from competition. These barriers to entry include: (1) ownership of an essential resource, (2) legal barriers, and (3) economies of scale.

2. A (an) _____ arises because of the existence of economies of scale in which the LRAC falls as production increases. As a result, smaller firms leave the industry, new firms fear competing with the monopolist, and the result is that a monopoly emerges naturally.

3. A firm that faces a downward-sloping demand curve is called a _____.

4. _____ allows the monopolist to increase profits by charging buyers different prices rather than a single price. There are three necessary conditions for this condition to exist: (1) the demand curve must be downward sloping, (2) buyers in different markets must have different demand curves, and (3) the buyer must be able to prevent _____ which is reselling the product at a higher price than the purchase price.

■ MULTIPLE CHOICE

1. Which of the following is a market structure of monopoly?

    a. Few firms operating as price takers.
    b. Single firm operating as a price taker.
    c. Single firm that is a price maker.
    d. All of the above are true.

2. A monopolist earns an economic profit only when:

    a. average total cost equals price.
    b. marginal cost equals price.
    c. marginal revenue equals price.
    d. average total cost is less than price.

3. Suppose a monopolist's demand curve lies below its average variable cost curve. The firm will:

    a. stay in operation in the short-run.
    b. earn an economic profit.
    c. earn an economic profit in the long run.
    d. shut down.

4.   Assume a monopolist charges a price corresponding to the intersection of the marginal cost and marginal revenue curves. If this price is between its average variable cost and average total cost curves, the firm will:

a.   earn an economic profit.
b.   assume demand will increase in the future.
c.   shut down.
d.   all of the above are true.

5.   Which of the following statements *best* describes the price, output, and profit conditions of monopoly?

a.   Price will equal marginal cost at the profit-maximizing level of output and profits will be positive in the long-run.
b.   Price will always equal average variable cost in the short-run and either profits or losses may result in the long run.
c.   In the long-run, positive economic profit will be earned.
d.   All of the above are true.

6.   Which of the following is a difference between a monopolist and a firm in perfect competition?

a.   The marginal revenue curve is downward-sloping.
b.   Marginal revenue equals price.
c.   Economic profits are zero in the long-run.
d.   The marginal revenue curve lies above the demand curve.

7.   At a price of $5, 24 units of the good would be sold; at a price of $7, 25 units of output would be sold. The marginal revenue of the 25th unit of output is:

a. $14.
b. $55.
c. $6.
d. $168.
e. $175.

Exhibit 1 Profit maximizing for a monopolist

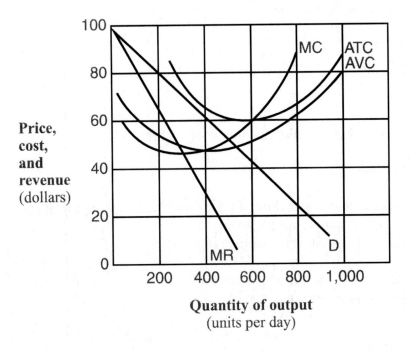

8.   In Exhibit 1, the profit-maximizing or loss-minimizing output for the monopolist is:

a.   200 units per day.
b.   300 units per day.
c.   400 units per day.
d.   500 units per day.
e.   600 units per day.

9.   In Exhibit 1, at the profit-maximizing or loss-minimizing output, the monopolist's total economic profit is:

a.   positive.
b.   negative.
c.   zero.
d.   minimum.

10.   In Exhibit 1, the monopolist would charge which of the following prices to maximize profit or minimize its loss?

a. $20.
b. $40.
c. $60.
d. $70.
e. $100.

11.   _____ is the act of buying a commodity in one market at a lower price and selling it in another market at a higher price.

    a.   Buying short.
    b.   Discounting.
    c.   Tariffing.
    d.   Arbitrage.

12.   Under both perfect competition and monopoly, a firm:

    a.   is a price taker.
    b.   is a price maker.
    c.   will shut down in the short-run if price falls short of average total cost.
    d.   always earns a pure economic profit.
    e.   sets marginal cost equal to marginal revenue.

13.   At the point at which the marginal revenue equals zero for a monopolist facing a straight-line demand curve, the total revenue is:

    a.   minimum.
    b.   maximum.
    c.   rising.
    d.   equal to zero.

14.   Which of the following is *true* for the monopolist?

    a.   Marginal revenue is less than the price charged.
    b.   Economic profit is possible in the long run.
    c.   Profit maximizing or loss minimizing occurs when marginal revenue equals marginal cost.
    d.   All of the above.

15.   For a monopolist to practice effective price discrimination, one necessary condition is:

    a.   identical price elasticity among groups of buyers.
    b.   differences in the price elasticity of demand among groups of buyers.
    c.   that the product is a homogeneous market.
    d.   None of the above.

16.   Suppose a monopolist's marginal revenue equals marginal cost at an output of 100. Suppose the price is $200, and average cost is $50 at an output of 100. Which of the following is correct about the monopolist's profit?

    a.   Profit = $250.
    b.   Profit = $150.
    c.   Profit = $15,000.
    d.   Profit = $50,000.
    e.   Profit = $250,000.

■ TRUE OR FALSE

1. T   F   A monopolist is a price searcher because it has the ability to select the price along its demand curve of its product.

2. T   F   Costs in a natural monopoly are lower because there is only one producer.

3. T   F   A natural monopoly maximizes profits at the point at which price equals minimum average total cost.

4. T   F   A monopolist that maximizes total revenue earns maximum economic profit.

5. T   F   Regardless of the demand for its product, a monopolist will be able to earn positive economic profits.

6. T   F   In order for a monopolist to earn a pure economic profit in short-run equilibrium, price must exceed average total cost.

7. T   F   To earn an economic profit in the short-run, a monopolist sets marginal revenue equal to zero.

8. T   F   An argument in favor of price discrimination is that this pricing strategy permits some consumers who otherwise would be excluded from a market to buy a good or service.

9. T   F   For a monopoly, price always equals marginal revenue.

10. T   F   Monopolies may earn economic losses in the long run.

■ CROSSWORD PUZZLE

Fill in the crossword puzzle from the list of key concepts. All of the concepts are not used.

ACROSS

2.   Buying low and reselling high.
4.   A _____ monopoly is an industry in which a single firm produces at a lower cost.
5.   A market with a single seller.

DOWN

1.   Different prices for the product.
3.   A firm facing a downward sloping demand curve is a price _____.

■ ANSWERS

Completion Questions

1. monopoly
2. natural monopoly
3. price maker

4. price discrimination, arbitrage

Multiple Choice

1. c 2. d 3. d 4. b 5. c 6. a 7. b 8. b 9. b 10. d 11. d 12. e 13. b 14. d 15. b 16. c

True or False

1. True 2. True 3. False 4. False 5. False 6. True 7. False 8. True 9. False 10. False

Crossword Puzzle

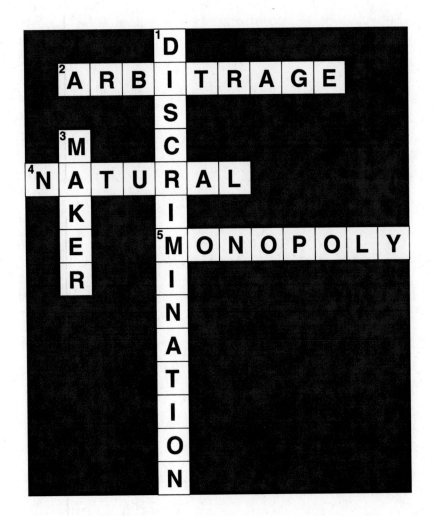

Chapter 9
Monopolistic Competition and Oligopoly

■ CHAPTER IN A NUTSHELL

This chapter discusses monopolistic competition and oligopoly. Monopolistic competition occurs when there are many sellers of a differentiated product and easy market entry and exit exists. As a result, the demand curve facing each firm slopes downward as under monopoly. The firm therefore produces less and charges a higher price than a firm under perfect competition. However, firms under monopolistic competition do produce a wider variety of products than under perfect competition. In the long-run, the result for each firm is zero economic profits, which is the same condition for perfect competition.

Oligopoly is characterized by a few firms selling either a homogeneous or differentiated product and entry for competitors is difficult. The result is firms operating with a great deal of mutual interdependence. This condition leads to three oligopoly models including: nonprice competition, price leadership, and the cartel. Nonprice competition is product differentiation, while price leadership involves one firm setting the price and the rest following their lead. A cartel is a formal agreement to control the price and output of a product, and game theory examines the strategic moves and countermoves of rivals.

■ KEY CONCEPTS

Cartel   Nonprice competition
Game theory   Oligopoly
Imperfect competition   Price leadership
Monopolistic competition   Product differentiation
Mutual interdependence

■ LEARNING OBJECTIVES

After completing this chapter, you should be able to:

1. Describe the characteristics of the monopolistically competitive and oligopoly market environments.
2. Understand that the key characteristic of the monopolistically competitive market is differentiation and in the oligopoly it is pricing interdependence.
3. Graphically express the demand curve facing firms operating in a monopolistically competitive and oligopoly market environment.
4. Graphically find the profit maximizing quantity to produce and explain why this output is the profit maximizing quantity.
5. Graphically determine the area representing any economic profits or losses.
6. Explain short-run economic profits may persist in the long run.
7. Describe some examples of nonprice competition.
8. Define what a cartel is and describe its behavior.
9. Understand what price leadership is and its role in an oligopoly.
10. Compare and contrast the pros and cons of each of the 4 market environments from society's perspective.

THE ECONOMIST'S TOOL KIT
Analyzing Monopolistic Competition

Step one: One possible short-run option is that the monopolistically competitive firm earns an economic profit. Note that the price corresponding to the intersection of the MC and MR curves is above the ATC curve.

Step two: A second possible short-run option is that the monopolistically competitive firm suffers a loss. Note that the price corresponding to the intersection of the MC and MR curves is below the ATC curve.

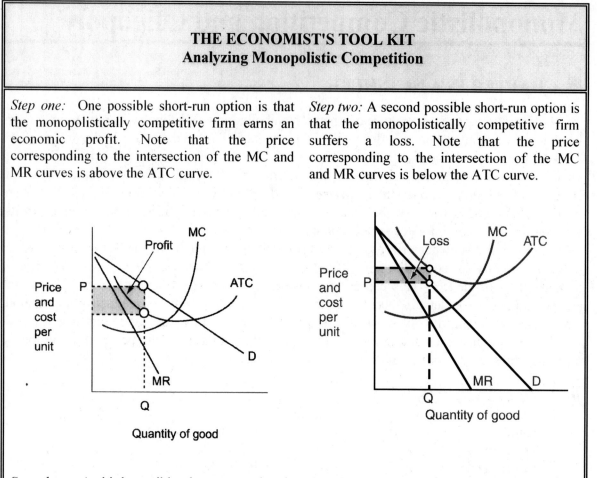

Step three: A third possible short-run option is that the monopolistically competitive firm shuts down. Note that the price corresponding to the intersection of the MC and MR curves is below the average variable cost curve (AVC).

Step four: In the long run, the monopolistically competitive firm earns zero economic profit. Note that the price corresponding to the intersection of the MC and MR curves equals the long-run average cost (LRAC).

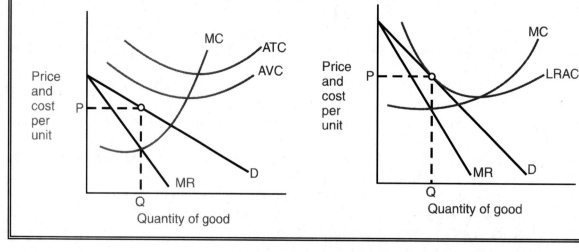

■ COMPLETION QUESTIONS

1. _____ is a market structure characterized by (1) many small sellers, (2) a differentiated product, and (3) easy entry and exit.

2. The process of creating real or apparent differences between goods and services is called _____.

3. Advertising, packaging, product development, better quality, and better service are examples of _____.

4. _____ is a market structure characterized by (1) few sellers, (2) a homogeneous or differentiated product, and (3) difficult entry.

5. _____ means an action by one firm may cause a reaction on the part of other firms.

6. The strategic moves and countermoves of rival firms can be explained using _____.

7. _____ occurs when a dominant firm in an industry raises or lowers its price, and other firms follow suit.

8. A (an) _____ is a formal agreement among firms to set prices and output quotas. The goal is to maximize profits, but firms have an incentive to cheat.

■ MULTIPLE CHOICE

1. Which of the following is a characteristic of the monopolistic competition market structure?

    a. Many firms and a homogeneous product.
    b. Few firms and differentiated products.
    c. Few firms and similar products.
    d. Few firms and a homogeneous product.
    e. Many firms and differentiated products.

2. Supporters of advertising claim that it:

    a. promotes the public interest.
    b. is a barrier to entry.
    c. allows new competitors a chance to gain market.
    d. all of the above.

3.   Critics of advertising argue that it:

    a.   lowers price by increasing competition.
    b.   results in more variety of products.
    c.   establishes brand loyalty, which promotes competition.
    d.   serves as a barrier to entry for new firms.

4.   The theory of monopolistic competition predicts that in long-run equilibrium a monopolistically competitive firm will:

    a.   produce the output level at which price equals long-run marginal cost.
    b.   operate at minimum long-run average cost.
    c.   overutilize its insufficient capacity.
    d.   produce the output level at which price equals long-run average cost.

5.   A monopolistic competitive firm is inefficient because the firm:

    a.   earns positive economic profit in the long run.
    b.   is producing at an output corresponding to the condition that marginal cost equals price.
    c.   is not maximizing its profit.
    d.   produces an output where average total cost is not minimum.

Exhibit 1 A monopolistic competitive firm

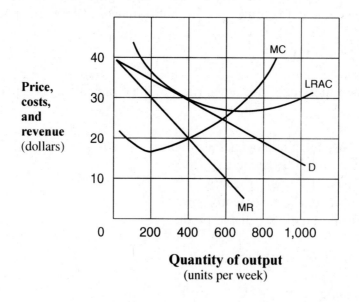

6.   As presented in Exhibit 1, the long-run profit-maximizing output for the monopolistic competitive firm is:

    a.   zero units per week.
    b.   200 units per week.
    c.   400 units per week.
    d.   600 units per week.
    e.   800 units per week.

7.   To maximize long-run profits, the monopolistically competitive firm shown in Exhibit 1 will charge a price per unit of:

    a.   zero.
    b. $10
    c. $20.
    d. $30.
    e. $40.

8.   As represented in Exhibit 1, the maximum long-run economic profit earned by this monopolistic competitive firm is:

    a.   zero.
    b. $10 per week.
    c. $4,000 per week.
    d. $40,000 per week.

9.   If all firms in a monopolistic competitive industry have demand and cost curves like those shown in Exhibit 1, we would expect that in the long run:

    a.   a number of new firms will enter the industry.
    b.   some firms will leave the industry.
    c.   firms in the industry earn zero economic profits.
    d.   all firms will leave the industry.

10.   Which of the following is a characteristic of an oligopoly?

    a.   Mutual interdependence in pricing decisions.
    b.   Independent pricing decisions.
    c.   Lack of control over prices.
    d.   All of the above are true.

11.   Which of the following is evidence that OPEC is an effective cartel?

    a.   Output changes are dictated by changes in demand.
    b.   Price changes are dictated by changes in demand.
    c.   Members do not agree on output quotas.
    d.   None of the above.

12.   An oligopoly is a market structure in which:

   a.   one firm has 100 percent of a market.
   b.   there are many small firms.
   c.   there are many firms with no control over price.
   d.   there are few firms selling either a homogeneous or differentiated product.

13.   Which of the following is *true* about an oligopoly equilibrium in comparison with equilibrium under similar circumstances but with perfect competition?

   a.   Output is larger and price is lower than under perfect competition.
   b.   Output is larger but price is higher than under perfect competition.
   c.   Output is smaller and price is higher than under perfect competition.
   d.   Output is smaller and price is lower than under perfect competition.

14.   A monopolistically competitive market is characterized by:

   a.   many small sellers selling a differentiated product.
   b.   a single seller of a product that has few suitable substitutes.
   c.   very strong barriers to entry.
   d.   mutual interdependence in pricing decisions.

15.   A monopolistically competitive firm will:

   a.   maximize profits by producing where MR = MC.
   b.   not likely earn an economic profit in the long run.
   c.   shut down if price is less than average variable cost.
   d.   all of the above.

16.   Which of the following is *true* about advertising by a firm?

   a.   It is not always successful in increasing demand for a firm's product.
   b.   It can increase demand and make demand more inelastic.
   c.   It may reduce per unit costs of production when economies of scale are experienced.
   d.   All of the above.

17.   An oligopoly:

   a.   and monopolistically competitive market produce less and charge higher prices than if their markets were perfectly competitive.
   b.   is characterized by mutual interdependence of pricing decisions.
   c.   may be characterized by price leadership.
   d.   all of the above.

18.   A cartel:

    a. is a group of firms formally agreeing to control the price and the output of a product.
    b. has as its primary goal to reap monopoly profits by replacing competition with cooperation.
    c. is illegal in the United States, but not in other nations.
    d. all of the above.

Exhibit 2 Two-Firm Payoff Matrix

		Texaco		
		High price		**Low Price**
Exxon	**High price**	A $30 billion $30 billion		B $10 billion $5 billion
	Low price	C $5 billion $10 billion		D $10 billion $10 billion

19.   Assume costs are identical for the two firms in Exhibit 2. If both firms were allowed to form a cartel and agree on their prices, equilibrium would be established by:

    a. Exxon charging the high price and Texaco charging the high price.
    b. Exxon charging the high price and Texaco charging the low price.
    c. Exxon charging the low price and Texaco charging the low price.
    d. Exxon charging the low price and Texaco charging the low price.

20.   Suppose costs are identical for the two firms in Exhibit 2. Each firm assumes without formal agreement that if it sets the high price its rival will *not* charge a lower price. Under these "tit-for-tat" conditions, equilibrium will be established by:

    a. Exxon charging the high price and Texaco charging the low price.
    b. Exxon charging the low price and Texaco charging the high price.
    c. Exxon charging the low price and Texaco charging the low price.
    d. Exxon charging the high price and Texaco charging the high price.

■ TRUE OR FALSE

1.   T   F   In the short run, the monopolistic competitive firm will charge a price equal to marginal cost.

2.   T   F   In a monopolistic competitive industry, short-run economic profit encourages entry of new firms until there are no economic profits in the long-run.

3.   T   F   In the long run, marginal cost must equal marginal revenue for a monopolistic competitive firm, but *not* at the minimum point of the long-run average cost curve.

4.   T   F   In an oligopoly, the outcome is uncertain because price and output decisions depend on the response of rivals.

5.   T   F   A cartel is an agreement among firms to divide output of a product among members.

6.   T   F   A major cartel problem is that member firms cheat by attempting to steal customers from one another.

7.   T   F   Cartels are generally legal in the United States.

8.   T   F   A monopolistic competitive firm in the long run sets price equal to the minimum point on the long-run average cost curve.

9.   T   F   Examples of nonprice competition include advertising and product differentiation.

10.   T   F   In order from the *most* to the *least* competitive market structure is the perfectly competitive, monopolistically competitive, monopolist and then the oligopolistic market structure.

■ CROSSWORD PUZZLE

Fill in the crossword puzzle from the list of key concepts. Not all of the concepts are used.

ACROSS

3. Advertising, packaging, better quality, and better service are examples of nonprice _____.

5. Product _____ is the process of creating real or apparent differences goods and services.

DOWN

1. Monopolistic competition and oligopoly belong to the _____ competition category.

2. _____ competition is a market structure characterized by many sellers, a differentiated product and easy market entry and exit.

3. A group of firms formally agreeing to control prices and output of a product.

4. A market structure characterized by few sellers.

■ ANSWERS

Completion Questions

1. monopolistic competition
2. product differentiation
3. nonprice competition
4. oligopoly
5. mutual interdependence
6. game theory
7. price leadership
8. cartel

Multiple Choice

1. e 2. c. 3. d 4. d 5. d 6. c 7. d 8. a 9. c 10. a 11. d 12. d 13. c 14. a 15. d 16. d 17. d 18. d 19. a 20. d

True or False

1. False 2. True 3. True 4. True 5. True 6. True 7. False 8. False 9. True 10. False

Crossword Puzzle

		¹I											²M	
		M		³C	O	M	P	E	T	I	T	I	O	N
		P		A									N	
		E		R				⁴O					O	
		R		T				L					P	
⁵D	I	F	F	E	R	E	N	T	I	A	T	I	O	N
		E		L				G					L	
		C						O					I	
		T						P					S	
								O					T	
								L					I	
								Y					C	

Chapter 10
Labor Markets and Income Distribution

■ CHAPTER IN A NUTSHELL

This chapter begins with a discussion of how the forces of supply and demand in a competitive labor market determine the wage rate. The firm's demand curve for labor is the firm's marginal revenue product (MRP) curve. The supply curve of labor is the relationship between the wage rate of labor and the quantity of labor supplied in the market. As a product's price is determined, the equilibrium wage rate is established by the intersection of the labor market supply and demand curves. Labor unions can increase the wage rate by increasing the demand for labor, decreasing the supply of labor, or collective bargaining.

The chapter ends with how wages and salaries are divided among members of society. The most widely accepted definition of poverty in the United States is computed by multiplying the cost of a minimal diet by 3 to get an income level that is used as the poverty line. The chapter concludes by explaining how discrimination in the workplace can cause certain groups to earn less than other groups not subjected to prejudice.

■ KEY CONCEPTS

Collective bargaining
Comparable worth
Demand curve for labor
Derived demand
Human capital

In-kind transfers
Marginal revenue product (MRP)
Poverty line
Supply curve of labor

■ LEARNING OBJECTIVES

After completing this chapter, you should be able to:

1. Understand that the market for labor is subject to the laws of demand and supply like any other market.
2. Calculate the marginal revenue product (MRP) of labor and derive a MRP of labor curve for a firm.
3. Understand that the market demand for labor curve is based on the MRP of labor for firms.
4. Describe what can cause a change in the market demand for labor.
5. Explain why a market supply of labor curve slopes upward and what can cause it to shift.
6. Describe the concept of derived demand.
7. Describe the impact of unions on wages and employment opportunities in those labor markets where they are present.
8. Describe in general terms the distribution of income in the U.S. and some of the causes of income distribution.
9. Describe what is meant by the poverty line and some causes of poverty.

10. Understand that any long-term solution to poverty must entail some investment in human capital.

11. Describe and distinguish cash transfer programs and in-kind transfers as antipoverty programs.

12. Describe what is meant by a comparable worth pay system.

■ COMPLETION QUESTIONS

1. _____ equals the price of the product times the worker's marginal product.

2. The _____ is the curve showing the different quantities of labor a firm is willing to hire at different prices of labor.

3. Changes in consumer demand for a product cause changes in demand for labor and other resources used to make the product. This concept is called _____ .

4. The _____ is the curve showing the different quantities of workers willing to work at different prices of labor.

5. The accumulated investment people make in education, training, experience, and health to make themselves more productive is called _____ .

6. _____ is the process of negotiations between the union and management over wages and working conditions.

7. The _____ is the level of income below which a person or a family is considered as being poor.

8. Government payments in the form of goods and services, rather than cash, including such government programs as food stamps, Medicaid, and housing are called

_____ .

9. _____ is the principle that employees who work for the same employer must be paid the same wage when their jobs, even if different, require similar levels of education, training, experience, and responsibility. It involves a non-market wage-setting process to evaluate and compensate jobs according to point scores assigned to different jobs.

■ MULTIPLE CHOICE

1. When a firm hires an additional unit of labor, the increase in a firm's total revenues is known as the marginal:

    a. cost.
    b. product.
    c. utility product.
    d. revenue product.

2. Assume Ajax Company employs 100 workers and total revenue is $400,000. When Ajax Company employs 101 workers, total revenue is $405,000. The marginal revenue product of the 101st workers is:

    a. $40 thousand.
    b. $5 thousand.
    c. $405 thousand.
    d. none of the above.

3. Assume consumer demand for CD-ROMs increases. The result is a (an):

    a. increase in derived demand for workers in the CD-ROM industry.
    b. increase in the marginal revenue product of firms in the CD-ROM industry.
    c. rightward shift in the market demand for labor curve in the CD-ROM industry.
    d. all of the above.
    e. none of the above.

4. Which of the following statements concerning the supply of labor is *true*?

    a. The supply of labor is determined by the prevailing wage rate.
    b. The labor supply curve is downward sloping.
    c. The wage rate has no effect on the supply of labor.
    d. None of the above.

5. One reason the supply of carpenters is greater than the supply of physicians is because:

    a. physicians do not belong to a union.
    b. carpenters demand less income.
    c. carpenters belong to unions.
    d. none of the above.

6.   Suppose a change in technology increases the marginal product of labor. The result is a (an):

    a.   leftward shift in the demand for labor curve.
    b.   rightward shift in the supply of labor curve.
    c.   downward movement along the demand for labor curve.
    d.   upward movement along the demand for labor curve.
    e.   none of the above.

7.   A firm's demand for labor depends on, in part, the demand for the firm's product. To summarize this idea, economists say that the demand for labor is:

    a.   derived demand.
    b.   marginal demand.
    c.   secondary demand.
    d.   monopsonistic demand.

8.   According to the statistics, the distribution of money income:

    a.   has not changed greatly since 1929.
    b.   changed significantly in favor of the top 5 percent since 1929.
    c.   fluctuated widely since 1947.
    d.   has not fluctuated greatly since 1947.

9.   The highest fifth of all families receive approximately _____ percent of the distribution of annual money income among families.

    a.   5.
    b.   10.
    c.   25.
    d.   75.
    e.   50.

10.   The official poverty line is defined as:

    a.   two times the cost of minimal food requirement.
    b.   one-third the average family income.
    c.   one-half the average family income.
    d.   none of the above.

11.   Which of the following might increase the supply curve of labor?

    a.   Increasing licensing requirements.
    b.   Increasing discrimination against females.
    c.   Increasing discrimination against blacks.
    d.   none of the above.

12.   Comparable worth is the principle that:

a.   men and women should be paid comparably.
b.   the wage rate equals the value of productivity.
c.   goods and services priced the same have about the same worth.
d.   employees who perform comparable jobs should be paid the same wage.

13.   Which of the following most closely represents the share of total U.S. income for the poorest 20 percent of all U.S. families?

a.   47 percent.
b.   23 percent.
c.   10 percent.
d.   4 percent.

14.   Which of the following are not counted when we compare a family's income to the poverty line?

a.   In-kind transfers such as food stamps, Medicaid, and public housing.
b.   Cash welfare payments such as from social security.
c.   Cash payments when a worker become unemployed.
d.   Both a. and b. above are correct.

15.   The poverty line:

a.   separates those on welfare from those not on welfare.
b.   equals three times an economy food budget.
c.   equals the median income level.
d.   all of the above.

16.   Which of the following statements is *true*?

a.   All people in poverty are on welfare.
b.   Unemployment compensation is an in-kind transfer.
c.   Temporary Assistance to Needy Families (TANF) is an example of a cash payment made by government to the impoverished.
d.   After cash assistance and in-kind transfers are considered, the distribution of income in the United States is more unequal.

17.   Which of the following government programs provides recipients with in-kind benefits?

a.   Temporary Assistance to Needy Families (TANF).
b.   Social Security.
c.   The food stamp program.
d.   Unemployment compensation.

18.   Consider a law that limits women's access to certain "dangerous" occupations like coal mining and military combat service. Such a law would likely reduce women's wages because:

a.   women would be overqualified for "non-dangerous" jobs.
b.   labor supply in female-intensive occupations would increase.
c.   women would be less likely to obtain college degrees.
d.   comparable worth would no longer exist between men's and women's occupations.

19.   Which of the following statements is *true*?

a.   Discrimination against women and blacks reduces the demand for these workers resulting in lower wages paid these workers.
b.   Discrimination is no longer a problem in the United States.
c.   A negative income tax system is a plan in which everyone pays the same percentage of their income as taxes.
d.   A negative income tax system is a plan where those below a certain income receive a cash payment from the government.

20.   Comparable worth is the principle that:

a.   goods and services priced the same have about the same worth.
b.   the wage rate equals the value of productivity.
c.   men and women should be paid comparably.
d.   employees who perform comparable jobs should be paid the same wage.

■ TRUE OR FALSE

1.   T   F   Marginal revenue product measures the addition to total revenue from selling an additional unit of a product.

2.   T   F   In a competitive labor market, marginal revenue product equals marginal product times the product price.

3.   T   F   In a competitive labor market, the demand for labor X that produces product Y will decrease if the demand for product Y increases.

4.   T   F   An increase in the demand for a product will shift the demand curve for labor producing the product to the right.

5.   T   F   An improvement in technology that increases the marginal product will shift the demand for labor curve to the left.

6.   T   F   One of the least economically effective ways to reduce poverty over time is through investment in human capital.

7.   T   F   Critics of an equal distribution of income argue that the effect would be to raise the incentive to be productive.

8.   T   F   Official figures indicate that the percentage of persons below the poverty level in the U.S. is more today than it was in 1965.

9.   T   F   When determining whether a family's income is below the official poverty line, non-cash benefits from the government, such as food, housing, and medical benefits, are not included.

10. T   F   The government defines poverty as an income level less than three times the cost of a minimal diet.

11. T   F   Wage discrimination means minority workers are paid unequal wages.

12. T   F   Discrimination raises the average wage of members of one group of workers in spite of laws that require equal pay for all workers.

■ CROSSWORD PUZZLE

Fill in the crossword puzzle from the list of key concepts. Not all of the concepts are used.

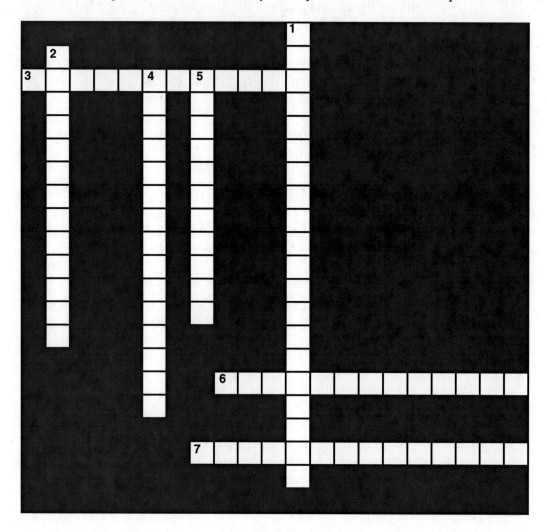

ACROSS

3.   The accumulation of education, training, experience, and health.

6.   Demand for labor depends on consumer demand.

7.   The quantity of labor employers hire at various wage rates.

DOWN

1.   The process of negotiations between union and management.

2.   The quantity of labor offered at different wage rates.

4.   Jobs requiring similar education, training, and experiences must be paid the same wage.

5.   The income below which a person or family is considered as being poor.

■ ANSWERS

Completion Questions

1. marginal revenue product (MRP)
2. demand curve for labor
3. derived demand
4. supply curve of labor
5. human capital
6. collective bargaining
7. poverty line
8. in-kind transfers
9. comparable worth

Multiple Choice

1. d 2. b 3. d 4. d 5. d 6. e 7. a 8. d 9. e 10. d 11. d 12. d 13. d 14. a 15. b 16. c 17. c 18. b 19. a 20. d

True or False

1. False 2. True 3. False 4. True 5. False 6. False 7. False 8. False 9. True 10. True 11. False 12. False

Crossword Puzzle

PART III
THE MACROECONOMY AND FISCAL POLICY

Chapter 11
Gross Domestic Product

■ CHAPTER IN A NUTSHELL

This chapter introduces you to national income accounting. It is important because it provides the foundation for understanding macroeconomics. The central macroeconomic variable is gross domestic product (GDP), which is the standard measure of the economy's output. The circular flow model separates GDP into markets for products, markets for resources, consumers spending and consumers earning money. Using the expenditure approach, GDP equals the total amount spent on final goods and services. Total spending (GDP) is broken down into four parts: consumption (C), investment (I), government spending (G), and net exports (X-M). National Income (NI), Personal Income (PI), and Disposable Personal Income (DI). The chapter concludes with an explanation for using the GDP deflator to calculate real GDP by removing inflation from nominal GDP.

■ KEY CONCEPTS

Circular flow model   Gross national product (GNP)
Disposable personal   Intermediate goods
income (DI)   National income (NI)
Expenditure approach   Nominal GDP
Final goods   Personal income (PI)
GDP chain price index   Real GDP
Gross domestic product (GDP)   Transfer payment

■ LEARNING OBJECTIVES

After completing this chapter, students should be able to:

1. Define GDP, GNP and describe the difference between the two.
2. Explain why only new and final goods and services are used in calculating GDP.
3. Express the circular flow nature of our economy.
4. Describe the components of GDP and their relative importance as a percentage of GDP.
5. List and describe some GDP shortcomings.
6. Calculate the other social accounts: NNP, NI, PI, and DI.
7. Explain the difference between nominal GDP and real GDP.
8. Calculate real GDP using a GDP chain price index.

■ COMPLETION QUESTIONS

1. _____ is the most widely used measure of a nation's economic performance and is the market value of all final goods produced in the United States during a period of time.

2. To avoid double counting, GDP does not include _____ .

3. The _____ is a diagram representing the flow of products and resources between businesses and households in exchange for money payments.

4. The _____ sums the four major spending components of GDP consisting of: consumption, investment, government, and net exports.

5. _____ is total income received by households and is calculated as national income less corporate taxes, retained earnings, Social Security taxes plus transfer payments and net interest from government securities.

6. _____ is personal income minus personal taxes.

7. _____ measures all final goods produced in a given time period valued at the prices existing during the time period of production.

8. _____ is the value of all final goods and services produced during any time period valued at prices existing in a base year.

9. A government payment to individuals not in exchange for goods or services currently produced is called a _____.

10. _____ are finished goods and services produced for the ultimate user.

11. The _____ is a measure that compares changes in the prices of all final goods during a given year to the prices of those goods in a base year.

■ MULTIPLE CHOICE

1. Gross domestic product (GDP) is defined as:

   a. the market value of all final goods and services produced within the borders of a nation.
   b. incomes received by all a nation's households.
   c. the quantity of each good and service produced by U.S. residents.
   d. none of the above.

2.   Gross domestic product (GDP) does *not* include:

    a.   used goods sold in the current time period.
    b.   foreign produced goods.
    c.   intermediate as well as final goods.
    d.   All of the above would *not* be included.

3.   The lower portion of the circular flow model contains factor markets in which households provide:

    a.   output of all final goods and services produced.
    b.   savings, spending, and investment.
    c.   labor, money, and machines.
    d.   land, labor, and capital.

Exhibit 1 Expenditure approach

National income account	(billions of dollars)
Personal consumption expenditures (C)	$1,000
Net exports (X-M)	100
Federal government consumption and gross investment expenditures (G)	200
State and local government consumption and gross investment expenditures (G)	400
Imports	20
Gross private domestic investment (I)	75

4.   As shown in Exhibit 1, total expenditures by households for domestically produced goods is:

    a. $1,000 billion.
    b. $100 billion.
    c. $600 billion.
    d. $20 billion.

5.   As shown in Exhibit 1, total expenditures by businesses for fixed investment (capital) and inventories is:

    a. $1,000 billion.
    b. $100 billion.
    c. $400 billion.
    d. $20 billion
    e. $75 billion.

6.   As shown in Exhibit 1, GDP is:

    a.   1,000.
    b.   1,500.
    c.   1,775.
    d.   2,000.

7.   GDP does count:

    a.   state and local government purchases.
    b.   spending for new homes.
    c.   changes in inventories.
    d.   none of the above.
    e.   all of the above.

8.   Personal income is:

    a.   national income minus transfer payments, net interest, and dividends.
    b.   the amount households have available only for consumption.
    c.   total income earned by households before taxes.
    d.   all of the above.
    e.   none of the above.

9.   The equation for determining real GDP for year X is:

    a. $\frac{\text{nominal GDP for year X}}{\text{average family income}} \times 100.$
    b. $\frac{\text{nominal GDP for year X}}{\text{GDP for year X}} - 100.$
    c. $\frac{\text{nominal GDP for year X}}{\text{average nominal GDP}}.$
    d.   none of the above.

10.   Suppose U.S. nominal GDP was $7,500 billion in Year X and the GDP chain price index is 120.0. Real GDP in constant Year X dollars is:

    a. $5,488 billion.
    b. $6,250 billion.
    c. $6,740 billion.
    d. $7,789 billion.

11.   If we computed GDP using the expenditure approach, and then computed it using the income approach, which of the following can be expected to be true?

    a.   GDP computed from the expenditure approach will be larger than when GDP is computed using the income approach.
    b.   GDP computed from the expenditure approach will be equal to GDP computed using the income approach.
    c.   GDP computed from the expenditure approach will be smaller than when GDP is computed using the income approach.
    d.   None of the above is correct.

12.   Which of the following correctly gives us national income (NI)?

    a.   Gross domestic product minus depreciation.
    b.   Personal income minus personal taxes.
    c.   Gross domestic product minus indirect business taxes.
    d.   Consumption plus investment plus government plus net exports.

13.   Which national income account should be examined to discover trends in the after-tax income that people have to save and spend?

    a.   Gross domestic product (GDP).
    b.   Gross national product (GNP).
    c.   National income (NI).
    d.   Disposable personal income (DI).

14.   Which of the following is a shortcoming of GDP?

    a.   GDP excludes changes in inventories.
    b.   GDP includes an estimate of illegal transactions.
    c.   GDP excludes nonmarket transactions.
    d.   GDP includes business investment spending.

15.   National income is officially measured by adding:

    a.   the quantity of each final good and service produced valued at its market price.
    b.   the total of all expenditures on newly produced final goods and services (GDP = C + I + H).
    c.   the total of all incomes earned by households from the sale of factors of production.
    d.   capital consumption allowance and gross domestic product (GDP + CCA = NNP).

16.   Which of the following is included in personal income but *not* in national income?

    a.   Compensation for workers.
    b.   Proprietors' income.
    c.   Corporate profits.
    d.   Social Security payments.
    e.   Rent.

Exhibit 2 GDP data (billions of dollars)

Personal consumption expenditures	$5,207.6
Interest	425.1
Corporate profits	735.9
Government spending	1,406.7
Depreciation	830.1
Rent	146.3
Gross private domestic investment	1,116.5
Compensation of employees	4,426.9
Exports	870.9
Imports	965.7
Indirect business taxes	553.1
Proprietors' income	520.3
Personal taxes	886.9
Social Security taxes	432.8
Transfer payments	376.6

17.   In Exhibit 2 and using the expenditures approach, gross domestic product (GDP) is:

    a. $6,807.6 billion.
    b. $7,082.9 billion.
    c. $7,636.0 billion.
    d. $7,637.7 billion.
    e. $7,730.8 billion.

18.   In Exhibit 2, and using the expenditures approach, national income (NI) is:

    a. $6,254.5 billion.
    b. $6,495.2 billion.
    c. $6,805.9 billion.
    d. $7,082.9 billion.
    e. $7,400.5 billion.

19.   In Exhibit 2, and using the expenditures approach, personal income (PI) is:

    a. $6,254.5 billion.
    b. $6,495.2 billion.
    c. $6,013.8 billion.
    d. $7,082.9 billion.
    e. $7,637.7 billion.

20.   In Exhibit 2, and using the expenditures approach, disposable personal income (DI) is:

    a. $5,126.9 billion.
    b. $5,608.3 billion.
    c. $6,254.5 billion.
    d. $6,495.2 billion.
    e. $7,082.9 billion.

■ TRUE OR FALSE

1.   T   F   Gross domestic product is the total dollar value at current prices of all final and intermediate goods produced by a nation during a given time period.

2.   T   F   The circular flow model illustrates that aggregate spending in the product markets equals 70 percent of aggregate income earned in the factor markets.

3.   T   F   Personal consumption expenditures is the largest component of total spending.

4.   T   F   Fixed investment is the dollar amount businesses are adding to our nation's amount of plant and equipment.

5.   T   F   Gross domestic product (GDP) is a satisfactory measure of both economic "goods" and "bads".

6.   T   F   The difference between gross domestic product and national income is an estimate of the depreciation of fixed capital.

7.   T   F   Nominal values are values measured in terms of the prices at which goods and services are actually sold.

8.   T   F   All changes in nominal GDP are due to price changes.

9.   T   F   If the GDP chain price index in a given year is less than 100, real GDP in that year would be greater than nominal GDP.

10.   T   F   A GDP price chain price index number of 120.0 for a given year indicates that prices in that year are 20 percent higher than prices in the base year.

11.   T   F   Over time, nominal GDP rises faster than real GDP because of the effects of inflation as measured by the GDP chain price index.

12.   T   F   In any year, nominal GDP divided by the GDP chain price index multiplied by 100 equals real GDP.

■ CROSSWORD PUZZLE

Fill in the crossword puzzle from the list of key concepts. Not all of the concepts are used.

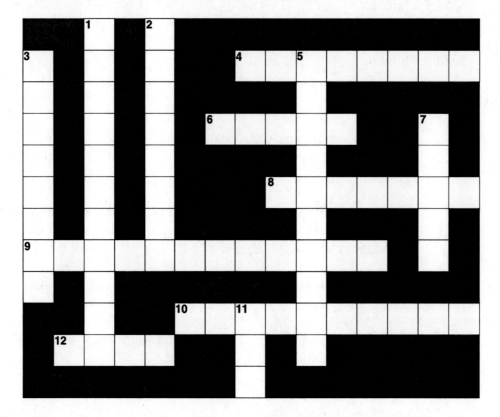

ACROSS

4.   _____ business taxes are levied as a percentage of the prices of goods sold and therefore collected as part of the firm's revenue.

6.   The _____ national product is the market value of all final goods and services produced by a nation's residents no matter where they are located.

8.   _____ GDP is the value of all final goods based on the prices existing during the time period of production.

9.   _____ goods and services used as inputs for the production of final goods.

10.   Finished goods and services produced for the ultimate user.

12.   _____ GDP is the value of all final goods produced during a given time period based on the prices existing in a selected base year.

DOWN

1.   _____ approach is a broad price index which measure changes in prices of consumer goods, business, construction, government spending, exports, and imports.

2.   The _____ flow model is a diagram showing the flow of products from businesses to households and the flow of resources from households to businesses.

3.   Gross _____ product is the market value of all final goods and services produced in a nation during a period of time usually a year.

5.   _____ personal income is the amount that households actually have to spend or save after payment of personal taxes.

7.   The GDP _____ price index is a measure that compares changes in the prices of all final goods during a given year to the prices of those goods in a base year.

11.   _____ is the gross domestic product minus depreciation of capital worn out in producing output.

■ ANSWERS

Completion Questions

1. gross domestic product (GDP)
2. intermediate goods
3. circular flow model
4. expenditure approach
5. personal income
6. disposable personal income
7. nominal GDP
8. real GDP
9. transfer payment
10. final goods
11. GDP chain index

Multiple Choice

1. a 2. d 3. d 4. a 5. e 6. c 7. e 8. e 9. d 10. b 11. b 12. c 13. d 14. c 15. c 16. d 17. c 18. c 19. c 20. a

True or False

1. False 2. False 3. True 4. True 5. False 6. True 7. True 8. False 9. True 10. True 11. True 12. True

Crossword Puzzle

Chapter 12
Business Cycles and Unemployment

■ CHAPTER IN A NUTSHELL

Over time real GDP rises and falls. These upswings and downswings are called the business cycle. Each cycle can be divided into four phases: peak, recession, trough, and expansion. Historical data is presented that shows the long-term trend in real GDP growth is about 3 percent since 1929. The government's chief forecasting gauge for business cycles is the index of leading indicators. The cause of the basic cycle is variation in total spending by households, businesses, government, and foreign buyers. Expressed as a formula: GDP = C + I + G + (X - M).

The text explains how to calculate the unemployment rate and then turns to some criticisms of the unemployment rate. The chapter concludes with a distinction between four types of unemployment: seasonal, frictional, structural, and cyclical. Full employment occurs when the unemployment rate is equal to the sum of the seasonal frictional and structural unemployment rates. The GDP gap is the difference between full-employment real GDP and actual real GDP.

■ KEY CONCEPTS

Business cycle
Coincident indicators
Cyclical unemployment
Discouraged worker
Economic growth
Frictional unemployment
Full unemployment
GDP gap
Labor force
Lagging indicators

Leading indicators
Offshoring
Outsourcing
Peak
Recession
Expansion
Structural unemployment
Trough
Unemployment rate

■ LEARNING OBJECTIVES

After completing this chapter, you should be able to:

1. Define what is meant by a business cycle and express it graphically.
2. Understand that changes in the business cycle are caused by changes in aggregate demand (total spending) and aggregate supply.
3. Describe the four phases of the business cycle.
4. Describe the problems associated with the recessionary and expansionary phases of the business cycle.
5. Understand that the long-term annual growth rate in real GDP in the U.S. is around 3%.
6. List some leading, coincident, and lagging economic indicators.
7. Define the full employment unemployment rate.

8.   Describe the different types of unemployment and realize that cyclical unemployment is associated with a recession.

9.   Define what is meant by a GDP gap and potential GDP.

■ COMPLETION QUESTIONS

1.   Recurrent rises and falls in real GDP over a period of years is called the _____.

2.   A (an) _____ is officially defined as two consecutive quarters of real GDP decline.

3.   _____ is measured by the annual percentage change in real GDP in a nation.

4.   Economic variables that change at the same time as real GDP changes are called _____.

5.   The nation's _____ consists of people who are employed plus those who are out of work but seeking employment.

6.   _____ are persons who want to work, but who have given up.

7.   _____ results from workers who are seeking new jobs that exist.

8.   _____ is unemployment caused by factors in the economy including lack of skills, changes in product demand, or technological change.

9.   _____ is unemployment resulting from insufficient aggregate demand.

10.   The _____ rate is equal to the total of the frictional and structural unemployment rates.

11.   The _____ is the difference between full-employment or potential real GDP and actual real GDP.

12.   The phase of the business cycle during which real GDP reaches its maximum after rising during an expansion is called a _____.

13.   A _____ is a phase of the business cycle during which real GDP reaches its minimum after falling during a recession.

14.   An upturn in the business cycle during which real GDP rises is called a _____ .

15.   _____ are variables that change before real GDP changes.

16. _____ is the percentage of people in the labor force who are without jobs and are actively seeking jobs.

17. Variables that change after real GDP changes are called _____.

■ MULTIPLE CHOICE

1. A business cycle is the period of time in which:

   a. a business is established and ceases operations.
   b. there are three phases which are: peak, depression, and expansion.
   c. real GDP declines.
   d. expansion and contraction of economic activity are equal.
   e. none of the above.

2. The _____ phase of the business cycle follows a recession.

   a. expansion.
   b. recession.
   c. peak.
   d. trough.

3. Variables that change before real GDP changes are measured by the:

   a. personal income index.
   b. real GDP index.
   c. forecasting gauge.
   d. index of leading indicators.

4. Which of the following is a lagging indicator?

   a. Outstanding commercial loans.
   b. Duration of unemployment.
   c. Prime rate.
   d. None of the above.
   e. All of the above.

5. The civilian labor force consists of:

   a. civilians who are not in prisons or mental hospitals.
   b. only individuals who are actually at work during a given week.
   c. all civilians over the age of 16.
   d. none of the above.

6.   A criticism of the unemployment rate is that:

a.   underemployment is measured in the calculation.
b.   the data includes part-time workers as fully employed.
c.   discouraged workers are included in the calculation.
d.   all of the above are problems.

7.   The number of people officially unemployed is *not* the same as the number of people who can't find a job because:

a.   people who have jobs continue to look for better ones.
b.   the armed forces is included.
c.   discouraged workers are not counted.
d.   none of the above.
e.   all of the above.

8.   Frictional unemployment refers to:

a.   unemployment related to the ups and downs of the business cycle.
b.   workers who are between jobs.
c.   people who spend relatively long periods out of work.
d.   people who are out of work and have no job skills.

9.   A mismatch of the skills of unemployed workers and the skills required for existing jobs is defined as:

a.   involuntary unemployment.
b.   cyclical unemployment.
c.   structural unemployment.
d.   frictional unemployment.

10.   Unemployment caused by a recession is called:

a.   structural unemployment.
b.   frictional unemployment.
c.   involuntary unemployment.
d.   cyclical unemployment.

11.   Full employment occurs when the rate of unemployment consists of:

a.   structural plus frictional unemployment.
b.   cyclical plus frictional unemployment.
c.   structural, frictional, and cyclical unemployment.
d.   none of the above.

12.   The GDP gap is the difference between:

    a.   frictional unemployment and actual real GDP.
    b.   unemployment rate and real GDP deflator.
    c.   full-employment real GDP and actual real GDP.
    d.   full-employment real GDP and real GDP deflator.

13.   A recession is a business contraction lasting at least:

    a.   one year.
    b.   six months.
    c.   three months.
    d.   one month.

14.   Which of the following is the correct formula for determining the civilian unemployment rate?

    a.   [(the number of unemployed, working-age civilians seeking work)/(the number of civilians in the labor force)] x 100.
    b.   C + I + G + (X-M).
    c.   The total number of unemployed, working-age civilians seeking work.
    d.   (The number of civilians in the labor force) x 100.

15.   When is the GDP gap largest?

    a.   During peak periods in the business cycle.
    b.   During trough periods in the business cycle.
    c.   When unemployment rates are relatively low.
    d.   When cyclical unemployment is close to zero.

16.   The natural rate of unemployment occurs if there is no:

    a.   unemployment.
    b.   frictional unemployment.
    c.   structural unemployment.
    d.   cyclical unemployment.

17.   Full employment is the situation in which the economy operates at an unemployment rate equal to the sum of:

    a.   structural, and frictional unemployment.
    b.   cyclical, and frictional unemployment.
    c.   structural and cyclical unemployment.
    d.   structural, frictional, and cyclical unemployment.

18.   Which of the following statements is *true*?

   a.   The four phases of the business cycle, in order, are: peak, expansion, trough, recession.
   b.   When unemployment is rising then real GDP is rising.
   c.   The economic problem typically associated with an expansion is rising unemployment.
   d.   Full employment exists in an economy when the unemployment rate equals the sum of frictional, and structural unemployment rates.

19.   The increase in unemployment associated with a recession is called:

   a.   structural unemployment.
   b.   frictional unemployment.
   c.   discouraged unemployment.
   d.   cyclical unemployment.
   e.   temporary unemployment.

20.   Of the four groups listed below, the highest unemployment rate is typically experienced by:

   a.   females as a group.
   b.   males as a group.
   c.   teenagers.
   d.   persons who completed 1-3 years of high school.

21.   Which of the following is a leading business cycle indicator?

   a.   The unemployment rate.
   b.   The volume of outstanding commercial loans.
   c.   New building permits.
   d.   Personal income.

■ TRUE OR FALSE

1.   T   F   Business cycles are recurring periods of economic growth and decline in an economy's real GDP.

2.   T   F   The term "expansion" refers to the maximum point of the business cycle.

3.   T   F   A person who has lost his or her job because it is now performed by a robot is structurally unemployed.

4.   T   F   Structural unemployment refers to short periods of unemployment needed to match jobs and job seekers.

5.   T   F   To be counted as unemployed, a person must be looking for a job.

6.   T   F   The civilian labor force includes only the employed.

7.   T   F   The official unemployment rate can be criticized for both understating and overstating the true number of unemployed.

8.   T   F   When actual real GDP output is below full-employment real GDP, the GDP measures the cost of cyclical unemployment.

9.   T   F   The natural rate of unemployment exists when cyclical unemployment equals zero.

10.   T   F   Full employment, which is always expected to occur, consists of the frictionally and cyclically unemployed.

■ CROSSWORD PUZZLE

Fill in the crossword puzzle from the list of key concepts. Not all concepts are used.

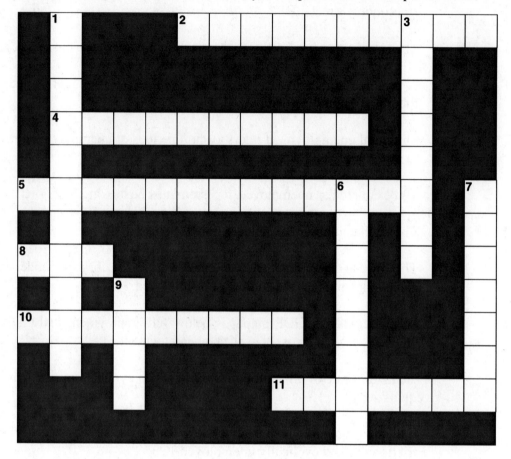

ACROSS

2.   _____ unemployment is caused by a mismatch of the skills of workers out of work and the skills required for existing job opportunities.

4.   _____ indicators are variables that change at the same time that real GDP changes.

5.   Alternating periods of economic growth and contraction.

8.   The GDP _____ is the difference between full-employment real GDP and actual real GDP.

10.   A downturn in the business cycle.

11.   The _____ indicators are variables that change before real GDP changes.

DOWN

1.   A _____ worker is a person not counted in the unemployment rate.

3.   An upturn in the business cycle.

6.   _____ unemployment is caused by the lack of jobs during a recession.

7.   _____ indicators are variables that change after real GDP changes.

9.   The phase of the business cycle during which real GDP reaches its maximum after rising during an expansion.

■ ANSWERS

Completion Questions

1. business cycle
2. recession
3. economic growth
4. coincident indicators
5. labor force
6. discouraged workers
7. frictional unemployment
8. structural unemployment
9. cyclical unemployment
10. full unemployment
11. GDP gap
12. peak
13. trough
14. expansion
15. leading indicators
16. unemployment rate
17. lagging indicators

Multiple Choice

1. e 2. d 3. d 4. e 5. d 6. b 7. c 8. b 9. c 10. d 11. a 12. c 13. b 14. a 15. b 16. d 17. a 18. d 19. d 20. c 21. c

True or False

1. True 2. False 3. True 4. False 5. True 6. False 7. True 8. True 9. True 10. False

Crossword Puzzle

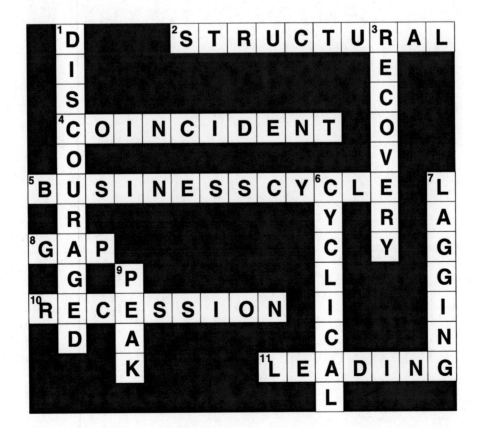

Chapter 13
Inflation

■ CHAPTER IN A NUTSHELL

This chapter explains how inflation is measured and the consequences of inflation. Inflation is a general upward movement in the price level. Changes in the price level are measured by the consumer price index (CPI) published by the Bureau of Labor Statistics. Unlike the GDP deflator, the CPI is based on a "market basket" of items purchased by a typical family. Between 1969 and 1982, the inflation rate averaged 7.6 percent. Since 1983, inflation has moderated and has averaged about 3 percent annually. Inflation can produce a redistribution of income and wealth. Real income adjusts nominal income for inflation. People whose nominal income does not rise faster than the rate of inflation lose purchasing power. Inflation can hurt lenders and savers when the real rate of interest is negative.

The chapter concludes with a discussion of demand-pull and cost-push inflation. Demand-pull occurs at or close to full employment. Cost-push inflation is the result of an increase in the costs of production. Finally, the chapter compares inflation in other countries and discusses the condition of runaway inflation.

■ KEY CONCEPTS

Base year
Consumer price index (CPI)
Cost-push inflation
Deflation
Demand-pull inflation
Disinflation
Hyperinflation

Inflation
Nominal income
Nominal interest rate
Real income
Real interest rate
Wage-price inflation spiral
Wealth

■ LEARNING OBJECTIVES

After completing this chapter, you should be able to:

1. Understand that inflation is a major problem most associated with the expansionary phase of the business cycle.
2. Understand what is meant by a consumer price index and know how it is calculated.
3. Describe the history of U.S. inflation rates in general terms.
4. Describe the consequences of inflation on real income, wealth and real interest rates.
5. Define the different types of inflation and distinguish between them.
6. Describe what is meant by hyperinflation.
7. Understand how demand-pull and cost-push inflation can feed on each other—wage-price inflation spiral.

■ COMPLETION QUESTIONS

1.   The _____ measures the cost of purchasing a market basket of goods and services by a typical household during a time period relative to the cost of the same bundle during a base year.

2.   During the early years of the Great Depression, the CPI declined at about a double-digit rate which is called _____.

3.   Between 1980 and 1986 _____ occurred. This does not mean that prices were falling, only that the inflation rate fell.

4.   To measure your purchasing power, requires converting _____ to _____ which adjusts for inflation.

5.   The _____ is the nominal interest rate adjusted for inflation.

6.   _____ is caused by pressure on prices originating from the buyers side of the market. On the other hand, _____ is caused by pressure on price originating from the sellers side of the market.

7.   _____ can cause serious disruptions to an economy by causing inflation psychosis, credit market collapses, a wage-price inflation spiral, and speculation.

8.   _____ occurs when increases in nominal wages cause higher prices and in turn higher wages and prices.

9.   An increase in the general (average) price level of goods and services in the economy is called _____.

10. The _____ is chosen as a reference point for comparison with some earlier or later year.

11. The value of the stock of assets owned at some point in time is called _____.

12. The _____ is the actual rate of interest earned over a period of time.

■ MULTIPLE CHOICE

1.   Inflation is measured by an increase in:

a.   homes, autos and basic resources.
b.   prices of all products in the economy.
c.   the consumer price index (CPI).
d.   none of the above.

2.   The consumer price index (CPI):

a.   adjusts for changes in product quality.
b.   includes separate market baskets of goods and services for both base and current years.
c.   includes only goods and services bought by the typical consumer.
d.   uses current year quantities of goods and services.

3.   Suppose a market basket of goods and services costs $1,000 in the base year and the consumer price index (CPI) is currently 110. This indicates the price of the market basket of goods and services is now:

a. $110.
b. $1,000.
c. $1,100.
d. $1,225.

Exhibit 1 Consumer Price Index

Year	Consumer Price Index
1	100
2	105
3	110
4	115
5	120

4.   As shown in Exhibit 1, the rate of inflation for Year 2 is:

a.   5 percent.
b.   10 percent.
c.   20 percent.
d.   25 percent.

5.   As shown in Exhibit 1, the rate of inflation for Year 5 is:

    a.   4.3 percent
    b.   5 percent.
    c.   20 percent.
    d.   25 percent.

6.   Disinflation means a decrease in the:

    a.   general level of prices in the economy.
    b.   prices of all products in the economy.
    c.   circular flow.
    d.   none of the above.

7.   Suppose the price of bananas rises over time and consumers respond by buying fewer bananas. This situation contributes to which bias in the consumer price index?

    a.   Substitution bias.
    b.   Transportation bias.
    c.   Quality bias.
    d.   Indexing bias.

8.   Which of the following is *correct*?

    a.   The percentage change in real income equals the percentage change in nominal income plus the percentage change in CPI.
    b.   Real income equals nominal income multiplied by the CPI as a decimal.
    c.   People whose nominal incomes rise faster than the rate of inflation lose purchasing power.
    d.   All of the above.
    e.   None of the above.

9.   Real income in 2000 is equal to:

    a.   Year X nominal income x CPI.
    b. $\dfrac{\text{Year X nominal income}}{\text{Year X real output}} \times 100.$
    c. $\dfrac{\text{Year X nominal income}}{\text{Year X real GDP}} \times 100.$
    d.   none of the above.

10.   If the rate of inflation in a given time period turns out to be higher than lenders and borrowers anticipated, then the effect will be:

    a.   a redistribution of wealth from borrowers to lenders.
    b.   a net gain in purchasing power for lenders relative to borrowers.
    c.   no change in the distribution of wealth between lenders and borrowers.
    d.   none of the above.

11.   Demand–pull inflation occurs:

   a.   when "too much money is chasing too many goods."
   b.   rising production costs.
   c.   during a recession.
   d.   all of the above.
   e.   none of the above.

12.   Cost–push inflation is due to:

   a.   "too much money chasing too few goods."
   b.   the economy operating at full employment.
   c.   increases in production costs.
   d.   all of the above.

13.   Suppose that your income during 2000 was $50,000, and the CPI for Year Y was 150 (base year = Year X) Back in Year X your income was $30,000. Has your real income increased or decreased from Year X to Year Y? By how much?

   a.   Increased by $5,000.
   b.   Increased by $3,333.33.
   c.   Unchanged.
   d.   Decreased by $3,333.33
   e.   Decreased by $5,000.

14.   If the bank offers you a nominal interest rate of 9 percent on a student loan, and if inflation is 6 percent, then what is the real interest rate?

   a.   15 percent.
   b.   9 percent.
   c.   6 percent.
   d.   3 percent.

15.   Consider borrowers and lenders who agree to loans with fixed nominal interest rates. If inflation is higher than what the borrowers and lenders expected, then who benefits from lower real interest rates?

   a.   Only the borrowers benefit.
   b.   Only the lenders benefit.
   c.   Both borrowers and lenders benefit.
   d.   Neither borrowers nor lenders.

16.   One way the consumer price index (CPI) differs from the GDP chain price index is that the CPI:

    a.   uses current year quantities of goods and services.
    b.   includes separate market baskets of goods and services for both base and current years.
    c.   includes only goods and services bought by typical urban consumers.
    d.   is bias free.

17.   As the price of gasoline rose during the 1970s, consumers cut back on their use of gasoline relative to other consumer goods. This situation contributed to which bias in the consumer price index?

    a.   Substitution bias.
    b.   Trasportation bias.
    c.   Quality bias.
    d.   Indexing bias.

18.   If the inflation rate exceeds the nominal rate of interest,

    a.   the real interest rate is negative.
    b.   lenders lose.
    c.   savers lose.
    d.   all of the above.

19.   Suppose you place $10,000 in a retirement fund that earns a nominal interest rate of 8 percent. If you expect inflation to be 5 percent or lower, then you are expecting to earn a real interest rate of at least:

    a.   1.6 percent.
    b.   3 percent.
    c.   4 percent.
    d.   5 percent.

20.   During the 1970s, the Organization of Petroleum Exporting Countries (OPEC) sharply increased the price of oil, which triggered higher inflation rates in the United States. This type of inflation is *best* classified as:

    a.   pseudo-inflation.
    b.   demand-pull inflation.
    c.   cost-push inflation.
    d.   hyperinflation.

■ TRUE OR FALSE

1. T   F   Inflation occurs when there is an increase in the purchasing power of money.

2. T   F   Unlike the GDP deflator, the CPI does not consider goods and services purchased by business and government.

3. T   F   Disinflation and deflation mean a decrease in the average price level.

4. T   F   A consumer price index of 110 for a given year indicates that prices in that year are 10 percent higher than prices in the base year.

5. T   F   If it cost $240 in Year X to buy the same market basket of goods that cost $120 in the base year, a consumer price index (CPI) for Year X, would have a value of 200.

6. T   F   If consumers reduce the purchase of goods whose relative prices rise (substitute bias), the consumer price index will tend to have an upward bias over time.

7. T   F   Changes in the quality of some goods and services, such as electromechanical calculators, are thought to give a downward bias to the consumer price index.

8. T   F   People with fixed incomes tend to fare best in an inflationary period.

9. T   F   Demand–pull inflationary pressure increases as the economy approaches full employment.

10. T   F   Cost–push inflation is caused by too much money chasing too few goods.

■ CROSSWORD PUZZLE

Fill in the crossword puzzle from the list of key concepts. Not all of the concepts are used.

ACROSS

1. The value of assets.
3. The _____ is an index that measures changes in the average prices of consumer goods and services.
6. _____ inflation is a rise in the price level caused by total spending.
8. A reduction in the rate of inflation.
9. A decrease in the average price level.
10. A _____ spiral is a situation that occurs when increases in nominal wage rates are passed on in higher prices, which, in turn, result in even higher nominal wage rates and prices.
11. _____ income is the actual dollars received over a period of time.

DOWN

2. An extremely rapid rise in the price level.
4. An increase in the average price level.
5. Income adjusted for inflation.
7. A year chosen as a reference point.

■ ANSWERS

Completion Questions

1. consumer price index (CPI)
2. deflation
3. disinflation
4. nominal income, real income
5. real interest rate
6. demand–pull inflation, cost–push inflation
7. hyperinflation
8. wage–price spiral
9. inflation
10. base year
11. wealth
12. nominal interest rate

Multiple Choice

1. c 2. c 3. c 4. a 5. a 6. d 7. a 8. e 9. d 10. d 11. e 12. c 13. b 14. d 15. a 16. c 17. a 18. d 19. b 20. c

True or False

1. False 2. True 3. False 4. True 5. True 6. True 7. False 8. False 9. True 10. False

Crossword Puzzle

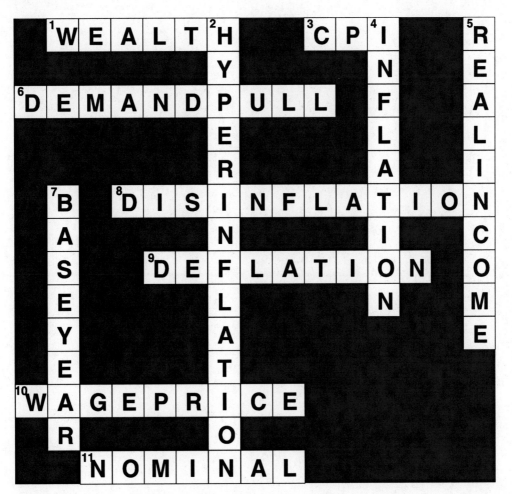

Chapter 14
Aggregate Demand and Supply

■ CHAPTER IN A NUTSHELL

The purpose of this chapter is to explain how the aggregate demand and aggregate supply curves determine the price level and the level of real GDP. The aggregate demand curve slopes downward because of the real balances effect, interest-rate effect, and net exports effect. As explained in chapter on GDP, determinates of the aggregate demand curve are consumption (C), investment (I), government purchases (G), and net exports (X-M). The aggregate supply curve slopes upward and consists of three ranges: Keynesian (horizontal segment), intermediate (rising segment), and classical (vertical segment). The equilibrium level of real GDP and the equilibrium price level are determined by the intersection of the aggregate demand and supply curves. The chapter ends by applying the aggregate demand and supply model to the concepts of demand-pull inflation and cost push inflation introduced in the previous chapter. For example, the text explains how a leftward shift in the aggregate supply curve caused by higher oil prices (cost-push inflation scenario) resulted in stagflation.

■ KEY CONCEPTS

Aggregate demand curve	Intermediate range
Aggregate supply curve	Keynesian range
Classical economists	Net exports effect
Classical range	Real balances or wealth effect
Interest-rate effect	Stagflation

■ LEARNING OBJECTIVES

After completing this chapter, you should be able to:

1. Understand that the use of the AD/AS model enables them to determine the equilibrium real GDP and price level as well as predicting the impact on real GDP and the price level given a change in either AD or AS.
2. Explain why the AD curve slopes downward in terms of the real balances or wealth effect, real interest-rate effect, and the net exports effect.
3. Interpret an increase (decrease) in AD and list what could cause this.
4. Explain why the AS curve takes on its slope through the three ranges.
5. Interpret an increase (decrease) in AS and list what could cause this.
6. Distinguish the Keynesian from the Classical position with respect to the macroeconomy in general terms.
7. Express demand-pull and cost-push inflation using AD and AS curves.
8. Express graphically and explain what is meant by stagflation.

THE ECONOMIST'S TOOL KIT
Developing the Aggregate Demand and Supply Model

Step one: Draw the aggregate supply curve (AS). In the Keynesian range, the price level is constant during a severe recession. In the intermediate range, the price level rises as full employment approaches. In the classical range, only the price level changes.

Step two: Include the aggregate demand curve (AD). Where the macroeconomic equilibrium occurs at point E, the equilibrium price level (P*) measured by a price index and equilibrium real GDP (Y*) is determined.

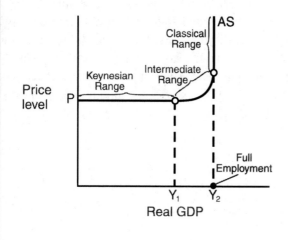

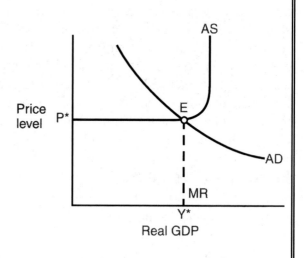

Step three: Demand-pull inflation results from an increase in aggregate demand beyond the Keynesian range. As AD₁ increases to AD₂, the price level rises from P₁* to P₂*.

Step four: Cost-push inflation results from a decrease in aggregate supply. As AS₁ decreases to AS₂, the price level rises from P₁* to P₂*.

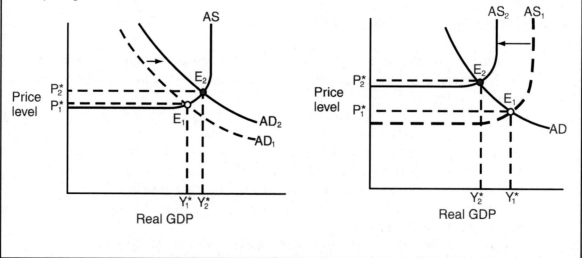

■ COMPLETION QUESTIONS

1.   The _____ shows the level of real GDP purchased in the economy at different price levels during a period of time.

2.   The _____ is the inverse relationship between the purchasing power of fixed-value financial assets and inflation which causes a shift in the consumption schedule.

3.   The _____ assumes a fixed money supply and, therefore, inflation increases the demand for money. As the demand for money increases, the interest rate rises causing consumption and investment spending to fall.

4.   The _____ is the inverse relationship between net exports and inflation. An increase in the U.S. price level tends to reduce U.S. exports and increase imports and vice versa.

5.   The _____ shows the level of real GDP that an economy produces at different possible price levels. The shape of the aggregate supply curve depends upon the flexibility of prices and wages as real GDP expands and contracts.

6.   The _____ of the aggregate supply curve is horizontal because neither the price level or production costs will increase with substantial unemployment in the economy.

7.   In the _____ of the aggregate supply curve, both prices and costs rise as real GDP rises toward full employment.

8.   The vertical segment of the aggregate supply curve is called the _____.

9.   _____ is an economy experiencing inflation and unemployment simultaneously.

10.   A group of economists who believed recessions would naturally be eliminated by the price system is called _____.

■ MULTIPLE CHOICE

1.   Which of the following is *not* a component of the aggregate demand curve?

    a.   Government spending (G).
    b.   Investment (I).
    c.   Consumption (C).
    d.   Net exports (X-M).
    e.   Saving.

2.   The interest-rate effect is the impact on real GDP caused by the direct relationship between the interest rate and the:

    a.   price level.
    b.   exports.
    c.   consumption.
    d.   investment.

3.   Which of the following could *not* be expected to shift the aggregate demand curve?

    a.   Net exports fall.
    b.   Consumption spending decreases.
    c.   An increase in government spending.
    d.   A change in real GDP.

4.   The pre-Keynesian or classical economic theory viewed the long-run aggregate supply curve for the economy to be:

    a.   backward bending at the full-employment level of real GDP.
    b.   positively sloped at the full-employment level of real GDP.
    c.   horizontal at the full-employment level of real GDP.
    d.   none of the above.

5.   Which of the following are beliefs of classical theory?

    a.   Long-run full employment.
    b.   Inflexible wages.
    c.   Inflexible prices.
    d.   All of the above.
    e.   None of the above.

6.   Assuming prices and wages are fully flexible, the aggregate supply curve will be:

    a.   upward sloping, but not vertical.
    b.   vertical.
    c.   horizontal.
    d.   downward sloping.

7. In the aggregate demand and supply model, the:

    a. aggregate supply curve is horizontal at full-employment real GDP.
    b. vertical axis measures real GDP.
    c. vertical axis measures the average price level.
    d. All of the above.
    e. None of the above.

8. Along the Keynesian range of the aggregate supply curve, a decrease in the aggregate demand curve will decrease:

    a. only the price level.
    b. only real GDP.
    c. both the price level and real GDP.
    d. real GDP and reduce the price level.

9. An increase in regulation will shift the aggregate:

    a. demand curve leftward.
    b. supply curve rightward.
    c. supply curve leftward.
    d. demand curve rightward.

10. An increase in the price level caused by a rightward shift of the aggregate demand curve is called:

    a. demand shock inflation.
    b. supply shock inflation.
    c. cost–push inflation.
    d. demand–pull inflation.

Exhibit 1 Aggregate supply and demand curves

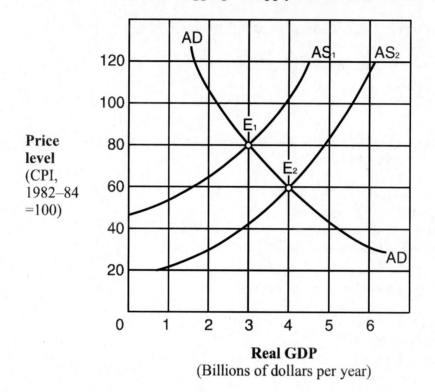

Real GDP
(Billions of dollars per year)

11.   A shift in the aggregate supply curve in Exhibit 1 from AS_1 to AS_2 would be caused by a (an):

    a.   decrease in input prices.
    b.   increase in input prices.
    c.   increase in real GDP.
    d.   decrease in real output.

12.   In Exhibit 1, the change in equilibrium from E_2 to E_1 represents:

    a.   cost–push inflation.
    b.   demand–pull inflation.
    c.   price–push inflation.
    d.   wage–push inflation.

13.   Keynes theorized that there are _____ when equilibrium real GDP is below the full employment level, which implies a _____ aggregate supply curve.

    a.   highly flexible prices and wages, vertical.
    b.   highly flexible prices and wages, horizontal.
    c.   fixed prices and wages, vertical.
    d.   fixed prices and wages, horizontal.

14.   In the intermediate range of the aggregate supply curve, if government expenditures increase caused the aggregate demand curve to shift outward, which of the following is most likely to occur?

   a.   The price level and real GDP will both rise.
   b.   The price level will not change, but real GDP will increase.
   c.   The price level will rise, but real GDP will not change.
   d.   Both the price level and real GDP will not change.

15.   _____ inflation can be explained by an _____ shift in the aggregate _____ curve.

   a.   Demand–pull, inward, demand.
   b.   Cost–push, outward, supply.
   c.   Demand–pull, outward, supply.
   d.   Cost–push, inward, supply.

16.   The net exports effect is the inverse relationship between net exports and the _____ of an economy.

   a.   real GDP.
   b.   GDP deflator.
   c.   price level.
   d.   consumption spending.

17.   The popular theory prior to the Great Depression that the economy will automatically adjust to achieve full employment is:

   a.   supply-side economics.
   b.   Keynesian economics.
   c.   classical economics.
   d.   mercantilism.

18.   Other factors held constant, a decrease in resource prices will shift the aggregate:

   a.   demand curve leftward.
   b.   demand curve rightward.
   c.   supply curve leftward.
   d.   supply curve rightward.

19.   Suppose workers become pessimistic about their future employment, which causes them to save more and spend less. If the economy is on the intermediate range of the aggregate supply curve, then:

   a.   both real GDP and the price level will fall.
   b.   real GDP will fall and the price level will rise.
   c.   real GDP will rise and the price level will fall.
   d.   both real GDP and the price level will rise.

20.   The concurrent problems of inflation and unemployment is termed:

    a.   depression.
    b.   downturn.
    c.   deflation.
    d.   demand-pull inflation.
    e.   stagflation.

21.   Which of the following correctly describes the aggregate supply curve?

    a.   A curve that shows the level of real GDP demanded at different possible price levels.
    b.   A curve that shows the level of real GDP produced at different possible price levels.
    c.   A curve that shows the level of quantity supplied by firms in a market at different possible prices, such as the supply of oranges in the oranges market.
    d.   None of the above.

22.   According to Keynesian theory, if equilibrium real GDP is below the full-employment level, then an increase in aggregate demand will result in which of the following changes in equilibrium?

    a.   Real GDP will rise, but the price level will remain constant.
    b.   Real GDP and the price level will both rise.
    c.   Real GDP will remain unchanged but the price level will rise.
    d.   None of the above.

23.   According to classical macroeconomic theory, if real GDP is below the full-employment level, then an increase in aggregate demand will result in which of the following changes in equilibrium?

    a.   Real GDP will rise, but the price level will remain constant.
    b.   Real GDP and the price level will both rise.
    c.   Real GDP will remain unchanged but the price level will rise.
    d.   None of the above.

■ TRUE OR FALSE

1.   T   F   The quantity of real GDP rises with the price level, ceteris paribus.

2.   T   F   The aggregate supply curve shows the relationship between the price level and the level of real GDP produced by the nation's economy.

3.   T   F   The interest-rate effect is the impact on real GDP caused by the inverse relationship between the price level and the interest rate.

4.   T   F   The net exports effect is the direct relationship between net exports and the price level of an economy.

5.   T   F   The Keynesian view is that the aggregate supply curve is vertical.

6.   T   F   The Classical economists believe that prices and wages quickly adjust to keep the economy operating at full employment.

7.   T   F   The Classical approach to a downturn in the business cycle was for the government to do nothing.

8.   T   F   If aggregate demand equals aggregate supply, macroeconomic equilibrium exists.

9.   T   F   An increase in input prices will cause the aggregate supply curve to shift rightward.

10.   T   F   A leftward shift in the aggregate supply curve along a fixed aggregate demand curve will cause cost–push inflation.

152   Chapter 14   Aggregate Demand and Supply

■ CROSSWORD PUZZLE

Fill in the crossword puzzle from the list of key concepts. Not all of the concepts are used.

ACROSS

3.   High unemployment and rapid inflation.
5.   The aggregate _____ curve represents the level of real GDP purchased by households, businesses, government, and foreigners.
6.   The _____ effect is the impact on total spending (real GDP) caused by the direct relationship between the price level and the interest rate.
7.   The _____ effect is the impact on total spending (real GDP) caused by the inverse relationship between the price level and the real value of financial assets with fixed nominal value.
8.   The _____ effect is the impact on total spending (real GDP) caused by the inverse relationship between the price level and the net exports of an economy.

DOWN

1.   The vertical segment of the aggregate supply curve.
2.   The _____ range is the rising segment of the aggregate supply curve.
3.   The aggregate _____ curve is the level of real GDP supplied by firms.
4.   The _____ range is the horizontal segment of the aggregate supply curve.

© 2013 Cengage Learning. All Rights Reserved. May not be scanned, copied or duplicated, or posted to a publicly accessible website, in whole or in part.

 **ANSWERS**

Completion Questions

1. aggregate demand curve
2. real balances or wealth effect
3. real interest-rate effect
4. net exports effect

5. aggregate supply curve
6. Keynesian range
7. intermediate range

8. classical range
9. stagflation
10. classical economists

Multiple Choice

1. e 2. a 3. d 4. d 5. a 6. b 7. c 8. b 9. c 10. d 11. a 12. a 13. d 14. a 15. d 16. c 17. c 18. d 19. a 20. e 21. b 22. a 23. c

True or False

1. False 2. True 3. False 4. False 5. False 6. True 7. True 8. True 9. False 10. True

Crossword Puzzle

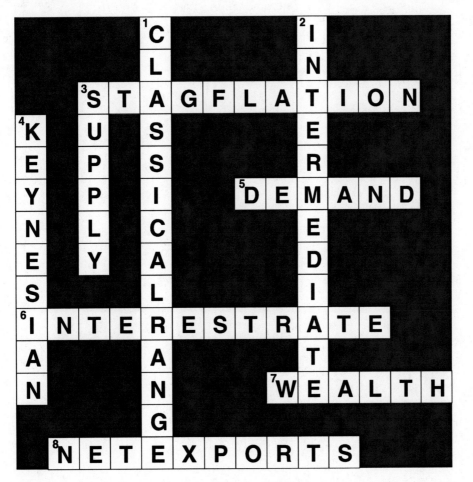

Chapter 15
Fiscal Policy

■ CHAPTER IN A NUTSHELL

The focus of this chapter is discretionary fiscal policy which involves changes in government purchases or taxes to shift the aggregate demand curve. When the economy suffers from high unemployment because GDP is below the full-employment, the government can follow expansionary fiscal policy and shift the aggregate demand curve rightward by increasing government spending and/or cutting taxes. When the economy suffers from inflation, the government can follow contractionary fiscal policy and shift the aggregate demand curve leftward by decreasing government spending and/or raising taxes. The spending multiplier amplifies the amount of the initial change in government spending, and the tax multiplier amplifies the amount of the initial change in taxes. Automatic stabilizers, such as automatic changes in transfer payments and tax revenues, can reduce variations in unemployment and inflation. The chapter concludes with a discussion of supply-side fiscal policy. According to this theory, government policy should shift the aggregate supply curve to the right by lowering taxes, which encourages work, savings, and investment.

■ KEY CONCEPTS

Automatic stabilizers	Laffer curve
Budget deficit	Marginal propensity to consume (MPC)
Budget surplus	Spending multiplier
Discretionary fiscal policy	Supply-side fiscal policy
Fiscal policy	Tax multiplier

■ LEARNING OBJECTIVES

After completing this chapter, you should be able to:

1.   Define fiscal policy.
2.   Define expansionary and contractionary fiscal policy and know when to use each over the course of the business cycle in order to smooth the business cycle out.
3.   Understand why the appropriate use of expansionary and contractionary fiscal policy will help moderate fluctuations in the business cycle.
4.   Calculate a spending and tax multiplier and explain why they exist.
5.   Understand that the spending multiplier exists no matter which component of total spending (aggregate expenditures) changes.
6.   Explain why any change in government spending has a more powerful impact on the economy than an equal but opposite change in taxes.
7.   Understand why deficits are recommended during recessions but budget surpluses are recommended during economic expansions.
8.   Explain why movement in the direction of a deficit (surplus) is expected to occur as the economy declines (expands) even though no deliberate action was taken to create this.

■ COMPLETION QUESTIONS

1. _____ follows the Keynesian argument that the federal government should manipulate aggregate demand to influence output, employment, and the price level in the economy.

2. The change in aggregate demand (total spending) resulting from an initial change in taxes is called the _____.

3. _____ are changes in taxes and government spending which occur in response to changes in the level of real GDP.

4. A (an) _____ occurs when government revenues exceed government expenditures. A (an) _____ occurs when government expenditures exceed government revenues.

5. _____ argues that lower taxes encourage work, saving, and investment which shift the aggregate supply curve rightward. As a result, output and employment increase without inflation.

6. The _____ represents the relationship between the amount of income tax revenue collected by the government and how much revenue will be collected at various tax rates.

7. The use of government spending and taxed to influence the nation's output, employment, and price level is called _____.

8. The _____ is an equal change in government spending and taxes, which changes aggregate demand by the amount of the change in government spending.

9. The multiplier by which an initial change in one component of aggregate demand, for example government spending changes aggregate demand (total spending) after an infinite number of spending cycles is called the _____ .

10. _____ is the change in consumption spending resulting from a change in income.

■ MULTIPLE CHOICE

1. Fiscal policy is concerned with:

    a. encouraging businesses to invest.
    b. regulation of net exports.
    c. changes in government spending and/or tax revenues.
    d. expanding and contracting the money supply.

2. Expansionary fiscal policy occurs when the government:

    a. increases its spending or increases its tax revenues.
    b. decreases its spending and increases its tax revenues.
    c. decreases its spending or reduces its tax revenues.
    d. none of the above.

3. If the marginal propensity to consume (MPC) is 0.80, the value of the spending multiplier is:

    a. 2.
    b. 5.
    c. 8.
    d. 10.

4. If the marginal propensity to save (MPS) is 0.25, the value of the spending multiplier is:

    a. 1.
    b. 2.
    c. 4.
    d. 9.

5. The formula to compute the spending multiplier is:

    a. 1/(C+I).
    b. 1/(1-MPS).
    c. 1/(MPC + MPS).
    d. 1/(1-MPC).

Exhibit 1 Aggregate demand and supply model

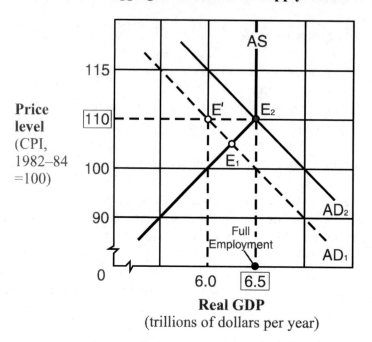

Real GDP
(trillions of dollars per year)

6.   Suppose the economy in Exhibit 1 is in equilibrium at point E_1 and the marginal propensity to consumer (MPC) is 0.75. Following Keynesian economics, the federal government can move the economy to full employment at point E_2 by:

    a.   decreasing government spending by $50 billion.
    b.   decreasing government spending by $200 billion.
    c.   increasing government spending by $125 billion.
    d.   decreasing government spending by $500 billion.
    e.   None of the above.

7.   Suppose the economy in Exhibit 1 is in equilibrium at point E_1 and the marginal propensity to consume (MPC) is 0.75. Following Keynesian economics, the federal government can move the economy to full employment at point E_2 by:

    a.   increasing government tax revenue by approximately $166 billion.
    b.   decreasing government tax revenue by $66 billion.
    c.   increasing government tax revenue by $500 billion.
    d.   decreasing government tax revenue by $500 billion.
    e.   decreasing government tax revenue by approximately $166 billion.

8.   Assume the marginal propensity to consume (MPC) is 0.90 and the government increases taxes by $100 billion. The aggregate demand curve will shift to the:

    a.   left by $1,000 billion.
    b.   right by $1,000 billion.
    c.   right by $900 billion.
    d.   left by $900 billion.
    e.   None of the above.

Exhibit 2 Aggregate demand and supply model

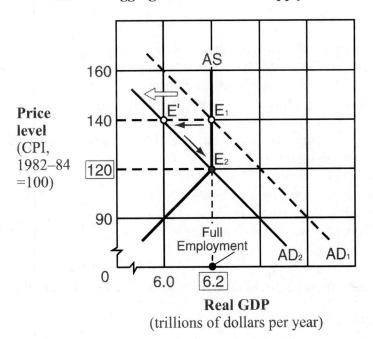

9.   Suppose the economy in Exhibit 2 is in equilibrium at point E_1 and the marginal propensity to consume (MPC) is 0.75. Following Keynesian economics, the federal government can move the economy to point E_2 and reduce inflation by:

    a.   increasing government spending by $50 billion.
    b.   decreasing government spending by $6 billion.
    c.   decreasing government spending by $100 billion.
    d.   decreasing government spending by $50 billion.
    e.   None of the above.

10.   Suppose the economy in Exhibit 2 is in equilibrium at point E_1 and the marginal propensity to consume (MPC) is 0.75. Following Keynesian economics, the federal government can move the economy to point E_2 and reduce inflation by:

    a.   increasing government tax revenue by $6 billion.
    b.   decreasing government tax revenue by $6.1 billion.
    c.   decreasing government tax revenue by $200 billion.
    d.   increasing government tax revenue by approximately $66 billion.
    e.   decreasing government tax revenue by approximately $66 billion.

11.   Automatic stabilizers tend to "lean against the prevailing wind" of the business cycle because:

    a.   wages are controlled by the minimum wage law.
    b.   federal expenditures and tax revenues change as the level of real GDP changes.
    c.   the spending and tax multiplier are constant.
    d.   special interests influence government spending and tax revenue legislation.

12.   In the U.S. economy, the effect on federal tax revenues and federal spending of a decrease in employment is to:

    a.   cut tax revenues and raise spending.
    b.   cut spending and raise tax revenues.
    c.   raise both tax revenues and spending.
    d.   cut both spending and tax revenues.

13.   An advocate of supply-side fiscal policy would advocate which of the following?

    a.   Subsidies to produce technological advances.
    b.   Reduction in regulation.
    c.   Reduction in resource prices.
    d.   Reduction in taxes.
    e.   All of the above.

14.   Which of the following favors government policies to stimulate the economy by creating incentives for individuals and businesses to increase their productive efforts?

    a.   Supply-side economics.
    b.   Keynesian economics.
    c.   Monetarist economics.
    d.   Marxian economics.

15.   Under the Laffer curve theory, changes in the federal tax rate affect:

    a.   tax revenue.
    b.   savings.
    c.   investment.
    d.   incentive to work.
    e.   All of the above.

16.   If the marginal propensity to consume (MPC) is 0.80, and if policy makers wish to increase real GDP by $200 million, then by how much would they have to change taxes?

    a.   -$240 million.
    b.   -$200 million.
    c.   -$180 million.
    d.   -$50 million.
    e.   -$40 million.

17.   Continuing the problem in question 16, if the MPC is still 0.80, and if the goal is to increase real GDP by $200 million, then by how much would government spending have to change to generate this increase in real GDP?

    a. $240 million.
    b. $200 million.
    c. $180 million.
    d. $50 million.
    e. $40 million.

18.   Suppose that the economy is operating in a full-employment equilibrium along the vertical section of the aggregate supply curve, but at a higher-than-necessary price level. If the aggregate demand curve must be reduced by $100 billion in order for the price level to decline by the desired 5 percent, and if the marginal propensity to consume is 0.75, then what change in taxes would generate the desired price reduction?

    a. $300 billion.
    b.   -$75 billion.
    c. $33.3 billion.
    d.   -$25 billion.

19.   Which of the following groups believes that the economy can achieve full employment without inflation through tax reductions, lower resource prices, and deregulation?

    a.   Classical school.
    b.   Keynesian school.
    c.   Neo-Keynesian school.
    d.   Rational expectations school.
    e.   Supply-side school.

20.   The Laffer curve shows as tax rates rise, tax revenue:

    a.   rises.
    b.   first rises, then falls, and then rises again.
    c.   falls.
    d.   first rises, and then falls.
    e.   remains at a constant level.

■ TRUE OR FALSE

1.   T   F   Fiscal policy is the management of aggregate demand through changes in government purchases and taxes.

2.   T   F   The greater the marginal propensity to consume in the economy, the smaller the spending multiplier.

3.   T   F   If the marginal propensity to consume is 0.80, the value of the spending multiplier will be 5.

4.   T   F   The tax multiplier is less than the spending multiplier regardless of the value of the marginal propensity to consume.

5.   T   F   Keynesian economics focuses on the role of aggregate spending in determining the level of real GDP.

6.   T   F   Using the aggregate demand and supply model, expansionary fiscal policy will have no effect on the price level but will restore full-employment GDP.

7.   T   F   Using the aggregate demand and supply model, increasing aggregate demand along the classical range of the aggregate supply curve will have no effect on real GDP or the price level.

8.   T   F   Automatic stabilizers are government programs that tend to push the federal budget toward surplus as the real GDP rises and toward deficit as the real GDP falls.

9.   T   F   Supply-siders believe that high tax rates are a disincentive to labor supply.

10.   T   F   The Laffer curve represents the relationship between real GDP and various possible tax rates.

■ CROSSWORD PUZZLE

Fill in the crossword puzzle from the list of key concepts. Not all of the concepts are used.

ACROSS

4. _____ stabilizers are sometimes referred to as non-discretionary fiscal policy.

5. A _____ emphasizes government policies that increase aggregate supply in order to achieve long-run growth in real output, full employment, and a lower price level.

7. _____ fiscal policy is the deliberate use of change in government spending or taxes to alter aggregate demand and stabilize the economy.

8. _____ policy is the use of government spending and taxes to influence the economy.

DOWN

1. A curve relating the relationship between tax rates and total tax revenues.

2. The change in total spending caused by a change in taxes.

3. The budget _____ is when government expenditures exceed revenues.

6. A budget _____ is when government revenues exceed expenditures.

ANSWERS

Completion Questions

1. discretionary fiscal policy
2. tax multiplier
3. automatic stabilizers
4. budget surplus, budget deficit
5. supply-side fiscal policy
6. Laffer curve
7. fiscal policy
8. balanced budget multiplier
9. spending multiplier
10. marginal propensity to consume (MPC)

Multiple Choice

1. c 2. d 3. b 4. c 5. d 6. c 7. e 8. d 9. d 10. d 11. b 12. a 13. e 14. a 15. e 16. d 17. e 18. c 19. e 20. d

True or False

1. True 2. False 3. True 4. True 5. True 6. False 7. False 8. True 9. True 10. False

Crossword Puzzle

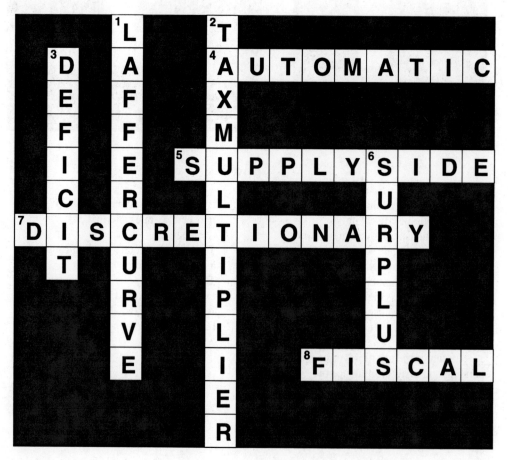

Chapter 16
The Public Sector

■ CHAPTER IN A NUTSHELL

The purpose of this chapter is to examine the economic role of the public sector and how it operates. The chapter begins with data on government spending and tax receipts classified into various categories. Since 1970 total government spending has been about one-third of GDP. The individual and social security taxes are important sources of federal tax revenues, and the sales and property taxes are important sources of state and local governments tax revenues. An interesting point is that citizens in the United States are taxed more lightly than citizens of many of the advanced industrial countries. The chapter also explains two basic tax characteristics-efficiency and equity. The two basic taxation philosophies of fairness are the benefits-received principles and the ability-to-pay principle. The chapter ends with a discussion of public choice theory, which considers how the government performs when it replaces the price system.

■ KEY CONCEPTS

Ability-to-pay principle   Progressive tax
Average tax rate   Proportional or flat-rate tax
Benefit-cost analysis   Public choice theory
Benefits-received principle   Rational ignorance
Government expenditures   Regressive tax
Marginal tax rate

■ LEARNING OBJECTIVES

After completing this chapter, you should be able to:

1.   Describe the major sources of government receipts and outlays at the federal, state and local levels as well as their trends.
2.   Explain what is at issue with respect to the difference between the efficiency versus the equity of taxation.
3.   Understand the "benefits-received" and the "ability-to-pay" principles with respect to the fairness of taxes issue.
4.   Distinguish between a progressive, proportional, and regressive tax based on the marginal tax rate on additional income.
5.   Describe the impact of a progressive, proportional, and regressive tax on after-tax income distribution.
6.   Describe some of the problems associated with government involvement as alluded to in the Public Choice Theory.

■ COMPLETION QUESTIONS

1.   The gasoline tax is a classic example of the_____ because users of the highways pay the gasoline tax.

2.   Progressive income taxes follow the _____ because there is a direct relationship between the average tax rate and income size. Sales, excise taxes, and flat-rate taxes violate this principle since each results in greater burden on the poor than the rich.

3.   The _____ is the tax divided by the income.

4.   The _____ is the fraction of additional income paid in taxes.

5.   A (an) _____ charges a higher percentage of income as income rises.

6.   A (an) _____charges a lower percentage of income as income rises.

7.   A (an) _____ charges the same percentage of income regardless of the size of income.

8.   _____ reveals the decision-making process involved in government. For example, government failure can occur because majority voting may not follow _____.

9.   _____ are federal, state, and local government outlays for goods and services, including transfer payments.

10.   The voter's choice to remain uninformed because the marginal cost of obtaining information is higher than the marginal benefit from knowing it is called _____.

■ MULTIPLE CHOICE

1.   Since 1950 total government expenditures in the United States:

   a.   grew from about one-quarter to about one-third of GDP.
   b.   fell by half, to 10 percent of GDP.
   c.   nearly doubled to one-half of GDP.
   d.   nearly tripled to about 60 percent of GDP.

2.   Currently, which of the following categories accounted for the largest percentage of total federal government expenditures?

    a.   Income security.
    b.   National defense.
    c.   Education and health.
    d.   Interest on the national debt.

3.   Currently, which of the following taxes contributed the greatest percentage of total federal government tax revenues?

    a.   Individual income taxes.
    b.   Corporate income taxes.
    c.   Social Security taxes.
    d.   Excise taxes.

4.   Which of the following countries devote the smallest percentage of its GDP to taxes?

    a.   Germany.
    b.   Sweden.
    c.   The United Kingdom.
    d.   The United States.

5.   "He who pays a tax should receive the benefit from the expenditure financed by the tax." This statement reflects which of the following principles for a tax?

    a.   Inexperience-to-collect.
    b.   Ability-to-pay.
    c.   Benefits-received.
    d.   Fairness of contribution.

6.   Jose pays a tax of $24,000 on his income of $60,000, while Richard pays a tax of $3,000 on his income of $30,000. This tax is:

    a.   a flat tax.
    b.   progressive.
    c.   proportional.
    d.   regressive.

7.   Which of the following can be classified as a regressive tax?

    a.   Excise tax.
    b.   Sales tax.
    c.   Gasoline tax.
    d.   All of the above.

8.   A tax is structured so that the tax as a percentage of income declines as the level of income increases is called a (an):

   a.   flat tax.
   b.   regressive tax.
   c.   progressive tax.
   d.   excise tax.

9.   Which of the following statements is *true*?

   a.   A sales tax on food is a regressive tax.
   b.   The largest source of federal government tax revenue is individual income taxes.
   c.   The largest source of state and local governments tax revenue is sales and excise taxes.
   d.   All of the above are true.
   e.   None of the above are true.

10.   Which of the following offers theories to explain why the government, like the private sector, may also "fail"?

   a.   Social economics.
   b.   Public choice theory.
   c.   Rational expectations theory.
   d.   Keynesian economics.

11.   People who often impose cost on the majority in order to benefit certain groups are called:

   a.   laissez-faire groups.
   b.   encounter groups.
   c.   fair-interest groups.
   d.   special-interest groups.
   e.   none of the above.

12.   The choice of a voter to remain uninformed because the marginal cost of obtaining information is greater than the marginal benefit from obtaining knowledge is called voter:

   a.   irrational ignorance.
   b.   rational ignorance.
   c.   collective interest.
   d.   choice.

13.   Total U.S. government expenditures as a percentage of GDP were largest during which of the following periods of time?

    a.   The Great Depression.
    b.   World War II.
    c.   The Vietnam War.
    d.   The Energy Crisis of the mid- and late-1970s.

14.   Suppose that society had been using a progressive income tax, but shifted to a proportional or true flat tax. If total tax revenues to government were the same under the two plans, who would be made better off and who would be made worse off?

    a.   Those with low incomes would be made better off, and those with high incomes would be made worse off.
    b.   People at all income levels would be better off.
    c.   People at all income levels would be worse off.
    d.   Those with low incomes would be made worse off, and those with high incomes would be made better off.

15.   Under majority rule, _____ can pass.

    a.   only those public projects that pass a benefit/cost test.
    b.   only those public projects that fail a benefit/cost test.
    c.   some public projects that fail a benefit/cost test.
    d.   no public projects.

16.   The major federal government expenditure is on:

    a.   national defense.
    b.   income security.
    c.   foreign aid.
    d.   the interest expense of the national debt.
    e.   none of the above.

17.   Sharon pays a tax of $4,000 on her income of $40,000, while Brad pays a tax of $1,000 on his income of $20,000. This tax is:

    a.   regressive.
    b.   progressive.
    c.   proportional.
    d.   a flat tax.

18.   Which of the following statements is *true*?

    a.   Sales, excise, and flat-rate taxes violate the ability-to-pay principles of taxation fairness because each results in a greater burden on the poor than the rich.
    b.   Government failure may occur if voters are rationally ignorant.
    c.   Government failure may occur because of special-interest group political pressure.
    d.   All of the above.

■ TRUE OR FALSE

1.   T   F   The term "public sector" refers only to federal government purchases of goods and services.

2.   T   F   The three major revenue sources for the federal government, in order of decreasing percentages, are individual income taxes, corporate taxes, and Social Security taxes.

3.   T   F   A person who is in a 31 percent marginal tax bracket and has a total taxable income of $100,000 will owe $31,000 in taxes.

4.   T   F   The federal income tax is progressive because the tax rates increase at higher income levels.

5.   T   F   State and local property taxes are regressive.

6.   T   F   Cost-benefit analysis can be applied to individual decision-making and to collective or public choice.

7.   T   F   A special interest group cannot impose its will on the majority because the perceived costs and benefits from government programs are the same for both groups.

8.   T   F   A rational person may remain less than fully informed on an issue to be decided in an election.

9.   T   F   Rational ignorance might explain low voter turnout because people apply marginal analysis to voting.

■ CROSSWORD PUZZLE

Fill in the crossword puzzle from the list of key concepts. Not all of the concepts are used.

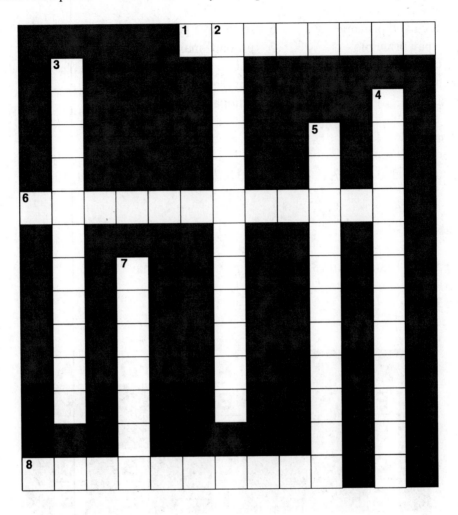

ACROSS

1. _____ ignorance is the voter's choice to remain uninformed because the marginal cost of obtaining information is higher than the marginal benefit from knowing it.

6. The _____ tax that charges rich and poor persons the same percentage of their income.

8. _____ expenditures are federal, state, and local outlays for goods and services.

DOWN

2. The _____ principle is the concept that the rich should pay a greater percentage of income in taxes.

3. A _____ tax charges rich persons a higher percentage of their income.

4. _____ theory is the analysis of government decision-making.

5. _____ analysis is the comparison of the additional rewards and costs of an alternative.

7. The _____ tax rate is the tax divided by income.

■ ANSWERS

Completion Questions

1. benefits-received principle
2. ability-to-pay principle
3. average tax rate
4. marginal tax rate
5. progressive tax
6. regressive tax
7. proportional tax
8. public choice theory, benefit-cost analysis
9. government expenditures
10. rational ignorance

Multiple Choice

1. a 2. a 3. a 4. d 5. c 6. b 7. d 8. b 9. d 10. b 11. d 12. b 13. b 14. d 15. c 16. b 17. b 18. d

True or False

1. False 2. False 3. False 4. True 5. True 6. True 7. False 8. True 9. True

Crossword Puzzle

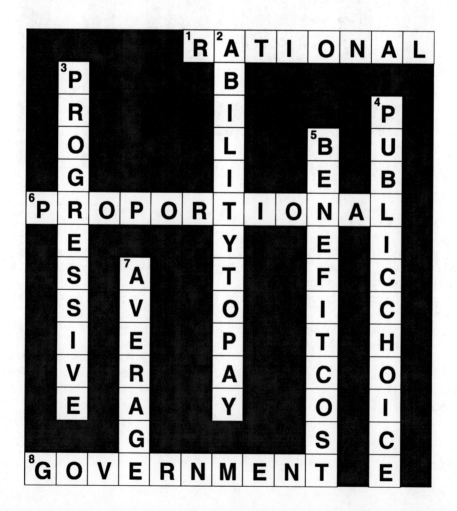

Chapter 17
Federal Deficits, Surpluses, and the National Debt

■ CHAPTER IN A NUTSHELL

The budget deficit is the difference between government expenditures, or outlays, and tax revenues. During the 1960s, the federal government was close to a balanced budget. During the early 1980s, federal budget deficits grew sharply and the public became very concerned about deficits. This situation changed when the federal government had budget surpluses beginning in 1998 and the Congressional Budget Office projected surpluses for years.

The national debt is the result of the federal government's borrowing to finance its deficits. Since 1975, the national debt has skyrocketed. Some measures to eliminate, or at least reduce, deficits include spending caps, the balance budget amendment and the debt ceiling. One reason for the concern over the national debt is the percentage of the debt held by foreigners. Paying foreigners interest and principal to finance the debt represents a transfer of wealth from U.S. citizens to citizens of other nations. Another concern is that the federal government's deficit spending might result in a cut in consumption and business investment because the government borrowing may push up the interest rate. In short, the fear is that government budget deficits may "crowd out" private spending.

■ KEY CONCEPTS

Crowding-out effect
Crowding-in effect
Debt ceiling
External national debt
Internal national debt
National debt

■ LEARNING OBJECTIVES

After completing this chapter, you should be able to:

1. Understand the stages through which fiscal policy must pass before it is enacted.
2. Describe the relationship between the deficit and the debt.
3. Cite some general historical trends with respect to the deficit and the debt.
4. Explain how deficits are financed and how this increases the national debt.
5. Critique some of the proposals to reduce the deficit.
6. List why we have a reason to worry and not to worry about whether the government can go broke, the question of whether we are passing the burden of the debt to our children, and whether there is a substantial crowding-out effect associated with deficit spending or not.
7. Describe what some potential problems are associated with the deficit and the debt and generally understand how these problems can be addressed.

■ COMPLETION QUESTIONS

1.   The _____ is the dollar amount that the federal government owes holders of government securities. It is the cumulative sum of past deficits.

2.   The percentage of the national debt a nation owes to its own citizens is called _____.

3.   _____ is a burden because it is the portion of the national debt a nation owes to foreigners. When interest is paid on this type of debt, this income transfers purchasing power to other nations.

4.   A burden of the national debt caused by the government borrowing to finance its deficit and causing the interest rate to rise is called the _____. As the interest rate rises, consumption and business investment falls.

5.   The _____ is the legislated legal limit on the national debt.

6.   The _____ is a theory that government capital spending offsets any decline in business investment resulting from government borrowing.

■ MULTIPLE CHOICE

1.   The federal budget process begins when federal agencies submit their budget requests to the:

   a.   Congressional Budget Office (CBO).
   b.   Council of Economic Advisors (CEA).
   c.   Department of Commerce (DOC).
   d.   Treasury Department.
   e.   None of the above.

2.   The sum of past federal budget deficits is the:

   a.   GDP debt.
   b.   trade debt plus GDP.
   c.   national debt.
   d.   Congressional debt.

3.   The U.S. Treasury financed federal budget deficits by selling:

   a.   Treasury bonds.
   b.   Treasury notes.
   c.   Treasury bills.
   d.   All of the above.
   e.   None of the above.

4.   Which of the following is *false*?

    a.   The national debt's size decreased steadily after World War II until 1980 and then increased sharply each year.
    b.   The national debt increases whenever the federal government has a surplus budget.
    c.   The size of the national debt currently is about the same size as it was during World War II.
    d.   All of the above are false.
    e.   All of the above are true.

5.   Between 1945 and 1980, the national debt as a percent of GDP:

    a.   increased substantially.
    b.   decreased substantially.
    c.   remained about the same.
    d.   increased slightly.
    e.   decreased slightly.

6.   Compared to Japan, the national debt as a percentage of GDP in the United States is:

    a.   substantially larger.
    b.   the same.
    c.   slightly larger.
    d.   substantially smaller.

7.   The national debt is unlikely to cause national bankruptcy because the:

    a.   national debt can be refinanced by issuing new bonds.
    b.   interest on the public debt equals GDP.
    c.   national debt cannot be shifted to future generations for repayment.
    d.   federal government cannot repudiate the outstanding national debt.

8.   Currently, the net interest payment as a percentage of GDP is:

    a.   about 5 percent.
    b.   less than 1 percent.
    c.   about 10 percent.
    d.   about 20 percent.

9.   Since 1990, net interest payments as a percentage of GDP has been:

    a.   increasing, but by such a small amount that it is not a matter of concern.
    b.   increasing.
    c.   constant.
    d.   decreasing.

10.   Which of the following U.S. Treasury securities represents internal ownership of the national debt?

a.   Bonds owned by private individuals.
b.   Bonds owned by the Social Security Administration.
c.   Bonds owned by the banks and insurance companies.
d.   All of the above.

11.   If all the national debt were owned internally, the federal government would not need to:

a.   worry about raising taxes to pay interest on the national debt.
b.   refinance the national debt.
c.   be concerned about the effect on the distribution of income from interest payments on the national debt.
d.   All of the above are true.
e.   None of the above are true.

12.   Which of the following statements about crowding out is *true*?

a.   It can completely offset the multiplier.
b.   It is caused by a budget deficit.
c.   It is not caused by a budget surplus.
d.   All of the above are true.
e.   None of the above.

13.   With regard to the national debt, to whom does the federal government owe money?

a.   Taxpayers.
b.   Federal government workers.
c.   The Treasurer of the United States.
d.   Investors who buy U.S. Treasury bills, bonds, and notes.

14.   If the national debt rises to the debt ceiling and there is currently a budget _____, then Congress and the President must agree to _____ the debt ceiling or else the federal government will have insufficient funds to pay its bills and will be forced to shut down.

a.   surplus, lower.
b.   deficit, raise.
c.   deficit, lower.
d.   none of the above.

15. Most of the U.S. national debt is owed to _____. Thus a rising national debt implies that there will be a future redistribution of income and wealth in favor of _____.

   a. foreigners, foreigners.
   b. other U.S. citizens, bondholders.
   c. foreigners, those needing government services.
   d. other U.S. citizens, those needing government services.

16. If Congress fails to pass a budget before the fiscal year starts, then federal agencies may continue to operate only if Congress has passed a:

   a. balanced budget amendment.
   b. deficit reduction plan.
   c. tax increase.
   d. continuing resolution.

17. The national debt is *best* described as the:

   a. amount by which this year's federal spending exceeds its taxes.
   b. value of all U. S. Treasury bonds owned by foreigners.
   c. sum of all federal budget deficits, past and present.
   d. percentage of GDP needed to finance a country's investment.

18. Which of the following statements is *true*?

   a. The national debt as a percentage of GDP is greater today than during any other period in our nation's history.
   b. A sizeable external national debt will transfer purchasing power away from foreigners to domestic citizens.
   c. Keynesian theory assumes a total crowding-out effect associated with deficit spending.
   d. U. S. national debt has more than tripled since 1980.

19. Crowding out occurs when the federal government:

   a. raises taxes to finance a budget deficit.
   b. refinances maturing U. S. Treasury bonds.
   c. borrows by selling bonds to finance a deficit.
   d. uses a budget surplus to pay off part of the national debt.

20. The crowding-out effect can be:

   a. zero.
   b. partial.
   c. complete.
   d. any of the above.

21.   When crowding out occurs, higher government spending results in higher interest rates, which in turn results in:

    a.   higher inflation.
    b.   less consumption and investment.
    c.   a larger debt ceiling.
    d.   more tax revenues.

■ TRUE OR FALSE

1.   T   F   The way to prevent the national debt from growing is for the budget not to be in deficit.

2.   T   F   When we speak of the national debt, we refer to the federal government debt only.

3.   T   F   The entire national debt is owed to U.S. citizens.

4.   T   F   Internal ownership of the debt refers to the portion of the national debt owned by government agencies.

5.   T   F   Less of the federal debt is owned by federal, state, and local governments than is owned by foreigners.

6.   T   F   Bonds owned by financial institutions represent ownership of the national debt by the private sector.

7.   T   F   External debt refers to the portion of the national debt owned by private individuals and internal debt refers to that part owned by the public sector.

8.   T   F   Increased government borrowing stimulates private borrowing because of its effect on interest rates.

9.   T   F   Less of the federal debt is owned by federal, state, and local governments than is owned by foreigners.

10.   T   F   An increase in a budget deficit financed by borrowing can increase interest rates and reduce investment spending thereby creating lower rates of economic growth.

■ CROSSWORD PUZZLE

Fill in the crossword puzzle from the list of key concepts. Not all of the concepts are used.

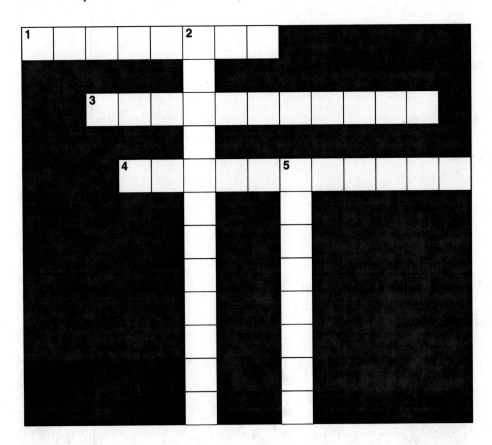

ACROSS

1. The _____ national debt is the portion of the national debt owed to foreigners.
3. The legislated legal limit on the national debt.
4. The _____ effect is a cut in private-sector spending caused by federal deficits.

DOWN

2. The total amount owed by the federal government.
5. The _____ national debt is the portion of the national debt citizens owe to themselves.

■ ANSWERS

Completion Questions

1. national debt
2. internal national debt
3. external national debt
4. crowding-out effect
5. debt ceiling
6. crowding-in effect

Multiple Choice

1. e 2. c 3. d 4. d 5. b 6. d 7. a 8. b 9. d 10. d 11. e 12. d 13. d 14. b 15. b 16. d 17. c 18. d 19. c 20. d 21. b

True or False

1. True 2. True 3. False 4. False 5. False 6. True 7. False 8. False 9. False 10. True

Crossword Puzzle

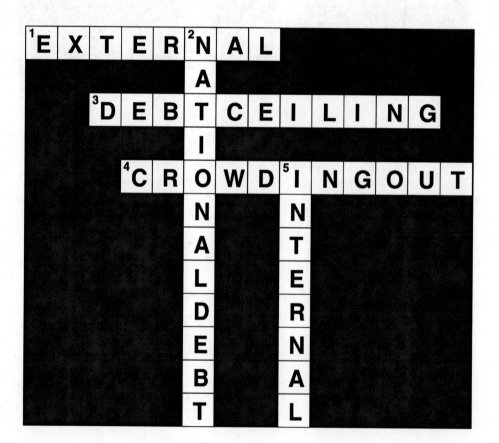

PART IV
MONEY, BANKING, AND MONETARY POLICY

Chapter 18
Money and the Federal Reserve System

■ CHAPTER IN A NUTSHELL

This chapter shifts the attention to money. Money performs these basic functions: it serves as a medium of exchange, a unit of account, and a store or value. Additional requirements are that money be scarce, portable, and divisible. Two measures of the money supply are M1 and M2. M1 is most narrowly defined money supply and it is equal to the sum of currency, traveler's checks, and checkable deposits. The chapter then moves to a discussion of the Federal Reserve System. The Fed is the institution responsible for regulating and controlling the money supply. Established in 1913, the Federal Reserve System is composed of a Board of Governors, 12 regional Federal Reserve Banks and commercial banks. The chapter ends with a discussion of the Monetary Control Act of 1980 that gives the Federal Reserve System greater control of nonmember banks.

■ KEY CONCEPTS

Barter	Federal Reserve System
Board of Governors	Fiat money
Checkable deposits	Medium of exchange
Commodity money	M1, M2
Currency	Money
Federal Deposit Insurance Corporation (FDIC)	Monetary Control Act
	Store of value
Federal Open Market Committee (FOMC)	Unit of account

■ LEARNING OBJECTIVES

After completing this chapter, you should be able to:

1.   Understand that money helps facilitate specialization and trade promoting economic activity.
2.   Describe the three functions of money.
3.   Explain why money must be relatively scarce and must be easily portable and divisible.
4.   Define M1, and M2 and understand that M2 is the definition used by the Fed to measure the money supply.
5.   Describe who runs the Fed and its institutional structure.
6.   List some of the Fed's functions.

7.   Understand that the Fed's primary function is to control the money supply.
8.   Understand that the FOMC undertakes open market operations and that open market operations are the principle way in which the Fed changes the money supply.
9.   Describe the Monetary Control Act of 1980 in general terms.
10.   Understand that banking is changing rapidly.

■ COMPLETION QUESTIONS

1.   _____ can be anything that serves as a (1) medium of exchange, (2) unit of account, and (3) store of value.

2.   _____ is the most important function of money. This means that money is widely accepted in payment for goods and services.

3.   _____ is the function of money to measure relative values by serving as a common yardstick for valuing goods and services.

4.   _____ is the property of money to hold its value over time. Money is said to be highly liquid, which means it is readily usable in exchange.

5.   _____ is money that has a marketable value, such as gold and silver. Today, the United States uses fiat money that must be accepted by law, but is not convertible into gold, silver, or any commodity.

6.   _____ is the narrowest definition of money which equals currency plus checkable deposits.

7.   _____ is a broader definition of money which equals M1 plus near monies, such as savings deposits and small time deposits.

8.   The _____ is our central bank and was established in 1913.

9.   The _____ directs the buying and selling of U.S. government securities, which is a key method of controlling the money supply.

10.   _____ is the direct exchange of one good for another good, rather than for money.

11.   Money accepted by law and not because of redeemability or intrinsic value is called _____.

12.   _____ is money, including coins and paper money.

13.   The total of checking account balances in financial institutions convertible to currency "on demand" by writing a check without advance notice is called _____.

14. _____ is   the
seven members appointed by the president and confirmed by the U.S. Senate who serve
for one nonrenewable 14-year term. Their responsibility is to supervise and control the
money supply and the banking system of the United States.

15. The _____ is
the government agency established in 1933 to insure commercial bank deposits up to a
specified limit.

16. A law, formally titled the Depository Institutions Deregulation and Monetary Control Act
of 1980, that gives the Federal Reserve System greater control of nonmember banks and
makes all financial institutions more competitive is called the _____.

■ MULTIPLE CHOICE

1. A direct exchange of fish for corn is an example of:

    a. storing value.
    b. a modern exchange method.
    c. barter.
    d. a non-coincidence of wants.

2. Which of the following is *not* an example of money used as a unit of account?

    a. A British pound is worth $3.00.
    b. Auto repairs for a small business were $3,000 and business travel was $8,000.
    c. A housewife has a $5,000 credit card limit.
    d. Gasoline sells for $1.20 per gallon and oil is $5.00 per quart.

3. Which of the following is a store of value?

    a. Money market mutual fund share.
    b. Repurchase agreement.
    c. All of the above are a store of value.
    d. None of the above are a store of value.

4. Anything can be money if it acts as a:

    a. unit of account.
    b. store of value.
    c. medium of exchange.
    d. All of the above.

5. Which one of the following statements is *true*?

    a. Money must be relatively "scarce" if it is to have value.
    b. Money must be divisible and portable.
    c. M1 is the narrowest definition of money.
    d. All of the above.

6.   Which of the following items is included when computing M1?

   a.   Checking accounting entries.
   b.   Currency in circulation.
   c.   Traveler's checks.
   d.   All of the above.
   e.   None of the above

7.   Which of the following is *not* part of M1?

   a.   Checking accounts.
   b.   Coins in circulation.
   c.   Credit cards.
   d.   Traveler's checks.
   e.   Paper currency in circulation.

8.   Which of the following is considered part of M2?

   a.   Savings deposits.
   b.   Money market mutual fund shares.
   c.   Small time deposits of less than $100,000.
   d.   All of the above.
   e.   None of the above.

9.   Members of the Federal Reserve Board of Governors serve one nonrenewable term of:

   a.   4 years.
   b.   7 years.
   c.   14 years.
   d.   life.

10.   Decisions regarding purchases and sales of government securities by the Fed are made by the:

   a.   FDIC.
   b.   Discount Committee.
   c.   Council of Economic Advisors.
   d.   Federal Funds Committee.
   e.   None of the above.

11.   Which of the following is *not* a protection against bank collapse?

   a.   The gold and silver that backs Federal Reserve notes.
   b.   The Federal Reserve Open Market Committee.
   c.   The Federal Deposit Insurance Corporation.
   d.   The Federal Reserve.

12.   The Monetary Control Act of 1980:

    a.   created less competition among various financial institutions.
    b.   allowed fewer institutions to offer checking account services.
    c.   restricted savings and loan associations to long-term loans.
    d.   all of the above.
    e.   none of the above.

13.   The difference between M1 and M2 is given by which of the following?

    a.   M1 includes paper currency, coins, gold and silver, whereas M2 does not contain gold and silver.
    b.   M1 is made up of currency, traveler's checks, and money in checkable accounts, whereas M2 contains M1 plus savings deposits and time deposits.
    c.   M1 is limited to currency, whereas M2 contains M1 plus traveler's checks and money in checkable accounts.
    d.   M1 includes currency and traveler's checks, whereas M2 contains M1 plus money in checking accounts.

14.   Suppose you transfer $1,000 from your checking account to your savings account. How does this action affect the M1 and M2 money supplies?

    a.   M1 and M2 are both unchanged.
    b.   M1 falls by $1,000 and M2 rises by $1,000.
    c.   M1 is unchanged, and M2 rises by $1,000.
    d.   M1 falls by $1,000 and M2 is unchanged.

15.   The use of a dollar bill to buy a concert ticket represents the use of money as a :

    a.   medium of exchange.
    b.   unit of account.
    c.   store of value.
    d.   all of the above.

16.   Which of the following is *not* a store of value?

    a.   Federal Reserve notes.
    b.   Credit card.
    c.   Debit card.
    d.   Passbook savings deposit.

17.   Which definition of the money supply includes credit cards?

    a.   M1.
    b.   M2.
    c.   M3.
    d.   None of the above includes credit card balances.

18.   The major protection against sudden mass attempts to withdraw cash from banks is the:

   a.   Federal Reserve.
   b.   Consumer Protection Act.
   c.   deposit insurance provided by the FDIC.
   d.   gold and silver backing the dollar.

19.   The number of presidentially appointed members who sit on the Federal Reserve Board of Governors is:

   a.   none.
   b.   seven.
   c.   nine.
   d.   twelve.

20.   The Federal Deposit Insurance Corporation (FDIC):

   a.   insures all demand deposit accounts up to $10 million in banks choosing FDIC protection.
   b.   was created as a government-owned corporation following the creation of the World Bank and the International Monetary Fund after World War II.
   c.   rarely evaluates bank performance to detect weaknesses in operation.
   d.   creates monetary policy in conjunction with the Federal Reserve Board.
   e.   was created to reduce the risk of banking by compensating depositors and keeping bank failures from spreading.

■ TRUE OR FALSE

1.   T   F   Money eliminates the need to barter.

2.   T   F   Any item can successfully serve as money.

3.   T   F   Money is said to be liquid because it is immediately available to spend for goods.

4.   T   F   M2 is actually a smaller amount than M1.

5.   T   F   The Federal Reserve System was created by act of Congress in 1931 in an effort to end a wave of bank failures brought on by the Great Depression.

6.   T   F   A majority of the commercial banks in the United States are members of the Fed.

7.   T   F   Although the chairman of its Board of Governors is appointed by the president, the Fed operates with considerable independence from the executive branch of the government.

8.   T   F   All banks are required to join the Fed.

9.   T   F   Although it has considerable political independence, the Fed is legally a branch of the U.S. Treasury Department.

10.   T   F   The Federal Funds Committee executes the purchases and sales of government securities decisions of the Federal Reserve.

■ CROSSWORD PUZZLE

Fill in the crossword puzzle from the list of key concepts. Not all of the concepts are used.

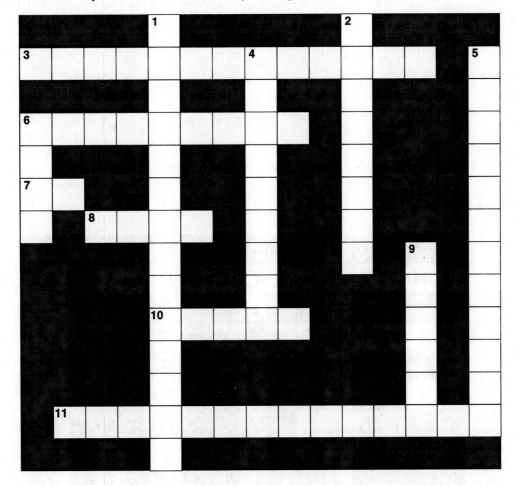

ACROSS

3.   The function of money to measure relative value.
6.   Money accepted by law.
7.   Currency, traveler's checks, and checkable deposits.
8.   A government agency established in 1933 to insure commercial bank deposits up to a specified limit.
10.   Anything that serves as a medium of exchange, unit of account, and store of value.
11.   The twelve central banks in the United States.

DOWN

1.   Anything that serves as money and also has market value.
2.   Coins and paper money.
4.   _____ deposits are checking account balances.
5.   The ability to hold money for future purchases.
6.   The committee that buys and sells U.S. securities to control the money supply.
9.   The direct exchange of goods and services.

■ ANSWERS

Completion Questions

1. money
2. medium of exchange
3. unit of account
4. store of value
5. commodity money
6. M1
7. M2
8. Federal Reserve System
9. Federal Open Market Committee (FOMC)
10. barter
11. fiat money
12. currency
13. checkable deposits
14. Board of Governors of the Federal Reserve System
15. Federal Deposit Insurance Corporation (FDIC)
16. Monetary Control Act

Multiple Choice

1. c 2. b 3. c 4. d 5. d 6. d 7. c 8. d 9. c 10. e 11. a 12. e 13. b 14. d 15. a 16. b 17. d 18. c 19. b 20. e

True or False

1. True 2. False 3. True 4. False 5. False 6. False 7. True 8. False 9. False 10. False

Crossword Puzzle

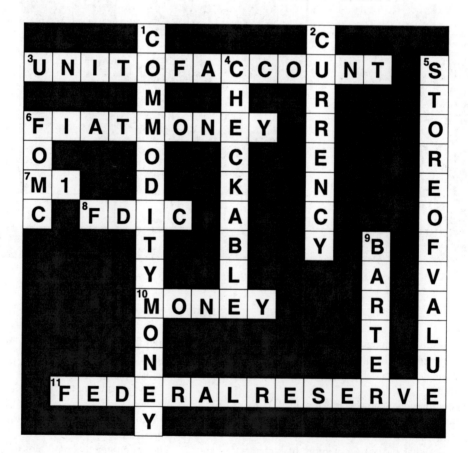

Chapter 19
Money Creation

■ CHAPTER IN A NUTSHELL

This chapter explains how the banking system creates money and thereby influences the money supply. The key to the money creation process is that banks practice fractional-reserve banking. This means banks keep only a fraction of their deposits on reserve as cash and deposits at the Federal Reserve. The minimum required reserves are required by law. A bank creates money by lending or investing its excess of required reserves. The money multiplier gives the maximum change in money (checkable deposits) due to a change in the excess reserves banks hold. The Federal Reserve uses monetary policy to change the money supply. The three basic monetary policy tools are: open market operations, changes in the discount rate, and changes in the required reserve ratio. For example, a sale of government securities by the Fed reduces reserves in the banking system and decreases the money supply. If the Fed wishes to increase the money supply, it might decrease the fraction of deposits that must hold on reserve.

■ KEY CONCEPTS

Discount rate   Money multiplier
Excess reserves   Monetary policy
Federal funds market   Open market operations
Federal funds rate   Required reserves
Fractional reserve banking   Required reserve ratio

■ LEARNING OBJECTIVES

After completing this chapter, you should be able to:

1. Understand that a private banking system can change the money supply whether the Fed desires it or not.
2. Explain what is meant by a fractional reserve banking system.
3. Define required reserves and excess reserves, and know how they are calculated.
4. Understand that a single bank cannot loan out any more funds than it has an excess reserves.
5. Explain how a single bank can create money (increase the money supply).
6. Calculate a money multiplier and explain how an entire banking system can increase and decrease the money supply by a multiple of its excess reserves.
7. Define monetary policy and explain what the monetary policy tools of the Fed are.
8. Explain what change would be required out of each of the three monetary policy tools of the Fed in order for the Fed to increase or decrease the money supply.
9. Explain the limitations of monetary policy that could render it relatively less effective.

■ COMPLETION QUESTIONS

1. _____ is the basis of banking today and originated with the goldsmiths in the middle ages.

2. The minimum balance that the Fed requires a bank to hold in vault cash or on deposit with the Fed is called the _____.

3. The percentage of deposits held as required reserves is called the _____ .

4. _____ allow a bank to create money by exchanging loans for deposits.

5. The _____ is the maximum change (positive or negative) in checkable deposits (money supply) due to a change in excess reserves.

6. Action taken by the Fed to change the money supply is called _____.

7. _____ are the buying and selling of government securities by the Fed through its trading desk at the New York Federal Reserve.

8. Changes in the _____ occur when the Fed changes the rate of interest it charges on loans of reserves to banks.

9. The _____ is a private market in which banks lend reserves to each other for less than 24 hours.

10. The interest rate banks charge for overnight loans of reserves to other banks is called _____.

■ MULTIPLE CHOICE

1. Which of the following appears on the asset side of a bank's balance sheet?

   a. Excess reserves.
   b. Loans.
   c. Required reserves.
   d. None of the above.
   e. All of the above.

2. Which of the following is an interest-bearing asset of commercial banks?

   a. Required reserves.
   b. Checkable deposits.
   c. Customer savings accounts.
   d. All of the above are interest-bearing assets of commercial banks.
   e. None of the above are interest-bearing assets of commercial banks.

3.   Which of the following is a valid statement?

    a.   Required-reserve ratio = required reserves as a percentage to total deposits.
    b.   Required reserves = the maximum reserves required by the Fed.
    c.   Excess reserves = total reserves plus required reserves.
    d.   All of the above.

4.   Tucker National Bank is subject to a 10 percent required-reserve ratio. If this bank received a new checkable deposit of $2,000, it could make new loans of:

    a. $200.
    b. $1,800.
    c. $2,000.
    d. $20,000.

5.   Tucker National Bank operates with a 20 percent required-reserve ratio. One day a depositor withdraws $500 from his or her a checking account at this bank. As a result, the bank's excess reserves:

    a.   fall by $500.
    b.   fall by $400.
    c.   rise by $100.
    d.   rise by $500.

6.   Assume a simplified banking system subject to a 25 percent required-reserve ratio. If there is an initial increase in excess reserves of $100,000, the money supply:

    a.   increases $100,000.
    b.   increases $400,000.
    c.   increases $125,000.
    d.   decreases $500,000.

7.   If the Fed wishes to increase the money supply then it should:

    a.   increase the required reserve ratio.
    b.   increase the discount rate.
    c.   buy government securities on the open market.
    d.   do any of the above.

8.   Decisions regarding purchases and sales of government securities by the Fed are made by the:

    a.   Federal Funds Committee (FFC).
    b.   Discount Committee (DC).
    c.   Federal Open Market Committee (FOMC).
    d.   Federal Deposit Insurance Commission (FDIC).

9.   The discount rate is the interest rate charged by:

   a.   banks for loans of less than 24 hours.
   b.   banks for overnight loans to other banks.
   c.   the prime rate plus one percent.
   d.   major banks to their best customers.
   e.   none of the above.

10.   The Monetary Control Act of 1980 extended the Fed's authority to:

   a.   impose required-reserve ratios on all depository institutions.
   b.   control the discount rate.
   c.   control the federal funds rate.
   d.   all of the above.

Exhibit 1 Balance sheet of Tucker National Bank

Assets		Liabilities	
Required reserves	$20,000	Checkable deposits	$200,000
Excess reserves	0		
Loans	180,000		
Total	$200,000	Total	$200,000

11.   The required-reserve ratio in Exhibit 1 is:

   a.   10 percent.
   b.   20 percent.
   c.   80 percent.
   d.   100 percent.

12.   Suppose Connie Rich deposits $100,000 into her checking account in the bank shown in Exhibit 1. The result would be a:

   a.   zero change in required reserves.
   b. $10,000 increase in required reserves.
   c. $100,000 increase in required reserves.
   d. $20,000 increase in excess reserves.

13. Assume the Fed purchases a government security from a private dealer and pays with a Fed check of $100,000. If this check is deposited by the dealer in the bank shown in Exhibit 1, the bank can extend new loans in the amount of:

   a. $20,000.
   b. $90,000.
   c. $100,000.
   d. $120,000.

14. Assume all banks in the system started with balance sheets as shown in Exhibit 1 and the Fed made a $20,000 open-market purchase. The result would be a (an):

   a. $200,000 expansion of the money supply.
   b. $20,000 expansion of the money supply.
   c. $20,000 contraction of the money supply.
   d. infinite contraction of the money supply.
   e. infinite expansion of the money supply.

15. _____ plus _____ plus _____ equals _____.

   a. Total deposits, loans, required reserves, excess reserves.
   b. Loans, required reserves, excess reserves, total deposits.
   c. Required reserves, total deposits, excess reserves, loans.
   d. Excess reserves, loans, total deposits, required reserves.

16. If total deposits at Last Bank and Trust are $100 million, total loans are $70 million, and excess reserves are $20 million, then which of the following is the required reserve ratio?

   a. 70 percent.
   b. 30 percent.
   c. 20 percent.
   d. 10 percent.

17. If Wilma sells a $10,000 Treasury bond to the Fed and deposits the money in her checking account, if the required reserve ratio is 10 percent, and if banks loan out all of their excess reserves, then what is the maximum increase in the money supply after the multiplier effect has fully operated?

   a. $1,000.
   b. $10,000.
   c. $100,000.
   d. $1,000,000.

18.   If the required reserve ratio is a uniform 25 percent on all deposits, the money multiplier will be:

    a.   4.
    b.   2.5.
    c.   0.75.
    d.   0.25.

19.   An increase in required-reserve ratio by the Federal Reserve would:

    a.   cause M1 to contract.
    b.   cause M1 to expand.
    c.   have no effect on M1 or M2.
    d.   affect only M2, not M1.

20.   Which of the following policy actions by the Fed would cause the money supply curve to increase?

    a.   An open-market sale.
    b.   An increase in required-reserve ratios.
    c.   A decrease in the discount rate.
    d.   All of the above.

■ TRUE OR FALSE

1.   T   F   Banks create money when they make loans.

2.   T   F   The required-reserve ratio is required reserves stated as a percentage of checkable deposits.

3.   T   F   In a system in which all banks have a uniform reserve requirement, the money multiplier is equal to 1 divided by the required-reserve ratio.

4.   T   F   In a simplified banking system, the money multiplier falls as the required-reserve ratio rises.

5.   T   F   As discussed in the text, a bank can extend new loans equal amount by which its excess reserves increase.

6.   T   F   An open-market purchase by the Federal Reserve injects excess reserves into the banking system and allows the money supply to expand.

7.   T   F   An increase in the discount rate by the Federal Reserve causes the money stock to expand.

8.   T   F   Banks that wish to borrow required reserves can turn to the federal funds market.

9.   T   F   The market in which banks make loans of reserves for terms of over one year is called the federal funds market.

10.   T   F   An increase in the required-reserve ratio by the Federal Reserve causes the money supply to contract.

■ CROSSWORD PUZZLE

Fill in the crossword puzzle from the list of key concepts. Not all concepts are used.

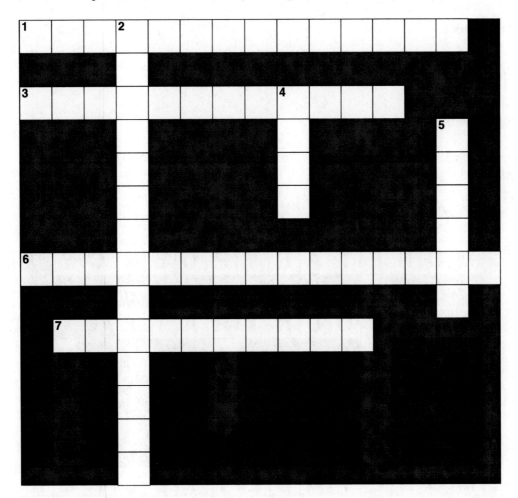

ACROSS		DOWN	
1.	The Fed's use of policy tools to change the money supply.	2.	Potential loan balances.
3.	The interest rate the Fed charges on loans of reserves to banks.	4.	The federal funds _____ is the interest rate banks charge for overnight loans of reserves.
6.	Equal to one divided by the required reserve ratio.	5.	The federal funds _____ is the market in which banks lend to each other for 24 hours.
7.	_____ operations is the buying and selling government securities by the Fed.		

■ ANSWERS

Completion Questions

1. fractional reserve banking
2. required reserve
3. required reserve ratio
4. excess reserves
5. money multiplier
6. monetary policy
7. open market operations
8. discount rate
9. federal funds market
10. federal funds rate

Multiple Choice

1. e 2. e 3. a 4. b 5. b 6. b 7. c 8. c 9. e 10. a 11. a 12. b 13. b 14. a 15. b 16. d 17. c 18. a 19. a 20. c

True or False

1. True 2. True 3. True 4. True 5. True 6. True 7. False 8. True 9. False 10. True

Crossword Puzzle

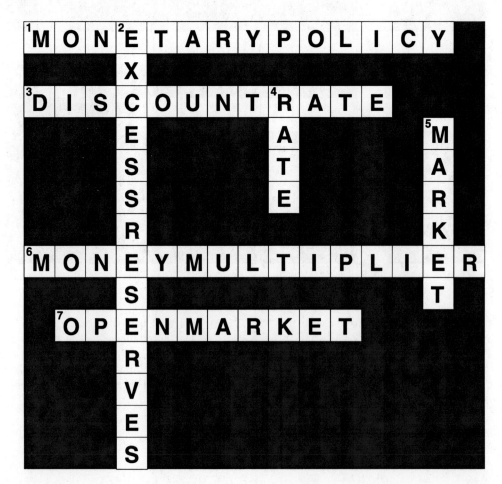

Chapter 20
Monetary Policy

■ CHAPTER IN A NUTSHELL

The previous two chapters provided the foundation for understanding the topic of this chapter: How changes in the money supply affect interest rates and, in turn, real GDP, employment, and the price level. The chapter begins with the Keynesian view that the downward-sloping demand for money curve is determined by these motives: transactions demand, precautionary demand, and speculate demand. The supply of money curve is represented by a vertical line because it is assumed to be established by the Fed regardless of the interest rate. The equilibrium interest rate occurs by the intersection of the money demand and the money supply curves. Assuming the demand for money curve remains fixed, the Fed can use its policy tools to change the interest rate by shifting the vertical money supply curve. In the Keynesian view, changes in the interest rate affects investment, aggregate demand, and, in turn prices, real GDP, and employment. In contrast, the monetarist transmission mechanism argues that changes in the money supply directly cause changes in the aggregate demand curve and thereby changes in prices, real GDP, and employment. Using the quantity theory of money, today's monetarists believe the Federal Reserve should increase the money supply by a constant percentage each year.

■ KEY CONCEPTS

Demand for money curve   Quantity theory of money
Equation of exchange   Speculative demand for money
Monetarism   Transactions demand for money
Precautionary demand for money   Velocity of money (v)

■ LEARNING OBJECTIVES

After completing this chapter, you should be able to:

1.   Define the transactions, precautionary, and speculative demand for money.
2.   Explain why the demand for money curve slopes downward and the supply of money curve is vertical.
3.   Explain how the interest rate reaches equilibrium and express this graphically.
4.   Explain how a change in the money supply affects the economy using a Keynesian framework.
5.   Describe the equation of exchange and the classical quantity theory of money.
6.   Explain how a change in the money supply affects the economy using the Monetarist framework.
7.   Describe how the Monetarists advocate using monetary policy.
8.   Compare and contrast the Classical, Keynesian and Monetarist schools of macroeconomic thought.

THE ECONOMIST'S TOOL KIT
Using Keynesian Monetary Theory

Step one: The money demand curve (MD) intersects the money supply curve (MS) at the equilibrium interest rate (i^*). An excess money demanded causes people to sell bonds, bond prices fall, and the interest rate rises. An excess money supplied causes people to buy bonds, bond prices rise, and the interest rate falls.

Step two: Here the Fed uses its tools to increase the money supply from MS_1 to MS_2 and causes a surplus at i_1^*. As a result, people buy bonds and the interest rate falls to i_2^* at an equilibrium quantity of money Q_2^*.

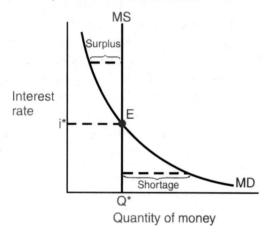

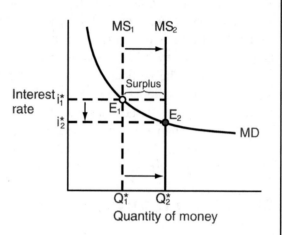

Step three: The Fed's action to lower the equilibrium interest rate from i_1^* to i_2^* causes a movement along the investment demand curve (I) from point A to point B. As a result, businesses increase investment spending from I_1 to I_2.

Step four: Since investment spending is a component the aggregate demand curve, the increase from I_1 to I_2 causes a rightward shift from AD_1 to AD_2. As a result, real GDP rises from Y_1^* to Y_2^* and the price level also rises.

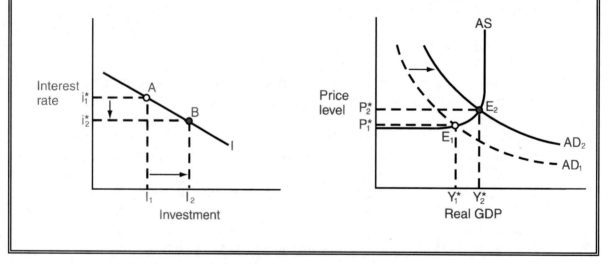

■ COMPLETION QUESTIONS

1. _____ is money held to pay for everyday predictable expenses.

2. _____ is money held to pay unpredictable expenses.

3. _____ is money held to take advantage of price changes in nonmoney assets.

4. The _____ shows the quantity of money people hold at various rates of interest.

5. _____ is the view that changes in monetary policy directly change aggregate demand, and thereby prices, real GDP, and employment.

6. The _____ is an accounting identity which is the foundation of Monetarism. The equation MV = PQ states that the money supply times the velocity of money is equal to the price level times real output.

7. The _____ is the number of times each dollar is spent. Keynesians view this concept as volatile and Monetarists disagree.

8. The _____ is a Monetarist argument that the velocity of money, V, and output Q, variables in the equation of exchange are relatively constant. Given this assumption, changes in the money supply yield proportionate changes in the price level.

■ MULTIPLE CHOICE

1. The stock of money people hold to pay everyday predictable expenses is the:

   a. transactions demand for holding money.
   b. precautionary demand for holding money.
   c. speculative demand for holding money.
   d. store of value demand for holding money.

2. The stock of money people hold to take advantage of expected future changes in the price of bonds, stocks, or other nonmoney financial assets is the:

   a. unit-of-account motive for holding money.
   b. precautionary motive for holding money.
   c. speculative motive for holding money.
   d. transactions motive for holding money.

3.   In a two-asset economy with money and T-bills, the quantity of money that people will want to hold, other things being equal, can be expected to:

    a.   decrease as real GDP increases.
    b.   increase as the interest rate decreases.
    c.   increase as the interest rate increases.
    d.   none of the above.
    e.   all of the above.

4.   Which of the following statements is *true*?

    a.   The speculative demand for money at possible interest rates gives the demand for money curve its upward slope.
    b.   There is an inverse relationship between the quantity of money demanded and the interest rate.
    c.   According to the quantity theory of money, any change in the money supply will have no effect on the price level.
    d.   All of the above.

5.   In Keynes's view, an excess quantity of money demanded causes people to:

    a.   sell bonds and the interest rate falls.
    b.   increase speculative balances.
    c.   buy bonds and the interest rate rises.
    d.   buy bonds and the interest rate falls.
    e.   none of the above.

6.   Assume the Fed decreases the money supply and the demand for money curve is fixed. In response, people will:

    a.   sell bonds, thus driving up the interest rate.
    b.   buy bonds, thus driving down the interest rate.
    c.   buy bonds, thus driving up the interest rate.
    d.   sell bonds, thus driving down the interest rate.

7.   Using the aggregate supply and demand model, assume the economy is operating along the intermediate portion of the aggregate supply curve. An increase in the money supply will increase the price level and:

    a.   raise the interest rate and lower real GDP.
    b.   raise both the interest rate and real GDP.
    c.   lower both the interest rate and real GDP.
    d.   have no effect on the interest rate and real GDP.
    e.   none of the above.

Exhibit 1 Money market demand and supply curves

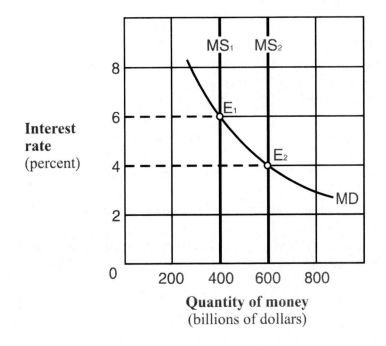

8. Starting from an equilibrium at E_1 in Exhibit 1, a rightward shift of the money supply curve from MS_1 to MS_2 would cause an excess:

    a. demand for money, leading people to sell bonds.
    b. supply of money, leading people to buy bonds.
    c. supply of money, leading people to sell bonds.
    d. demand for money, leading people to buy bonds.

9. As shown in Exhibit 1, assume the money supply curve shifts rightward from MS_1 to MS_2 and the economy is operating along the intermediate segment of the aggregate supply curve. The result will be a:

    a. higher interest rate and no effect on real GDP or the price level.
    b. lower investment, lower real GDP, and lower price level.
    c. higher investment, higher real GDP, and higher price level.
    d. higher investment, lower real GDP, and lower price level.

10. The equation of exchange states:

    a. $MV = PQ$.
    b. $MP = VQ$.
    c. $MP = V/Q$.
    d. $V = M/PQ$.

11.   The quantity theory of money of the Classical economists says that a change in the money supply will produce a:

a.   proportional change in the price level.
b.   wide variation in the velocity of money.
c.   less than proportional change in the price level.
d.   greater than proportional change in the price level.

12.   According to Keynesians, an increase in the money supply will:

a.   decrease the interest rate, and increase investment, aggregate demand, prices, real GDP, and employment.
b.   decrease the interest rate, and decrease investment, aggregate demand, prices, real GDP, and employment.
c.   increase the interest rate, and decrease investment, aggregate demand, prices, real GDP, and employment.
d.   only increases prices.

13.   Which of the following is *true*?

a.   Keynesians advocate increasing the money supply during economic recessions but decreaseing the money supply during economic expansions.
b.   Monetarists advocate increasing the money supply by a constant rate year after year.
c.   Keynesians argue that the crowding-out effect is rather insignificant.
d.   Monetarists argue that the crowding-out effect is rather large.
e.   All of the above.

14.   If the Fed reduces the discount rate, which of the following are *most* likely to result?

a.   The money supply shifts outward, and equilibrium interest rates fall in the money market.
b.   Investment declines, causing the aggregate demand curve to shift inward to the left, reducing equilibrium real GDP and thus slowing the economy.
c.   Investment rises, causing the aggregate demand curve to shift outward to the right, increasing equilibrium real GDP and thus accelerating the economy.
d.   Both a. and b. above are correct.
e.   Both a. and c. above are correct.

15.   If nominal GDP is $7 trillion, and the money supply is $2 trillion, then what is the velocity of money?

a.   14.
b.   7.
c.   3.5.
d.   2.

16.   How is modern monetarism different from Keynesianism?

    a.   Monetarists believe that inflation is caused by excessive growth in the money supply, based on the equation of exchange, while Keynesians believe that inflation is caused by excessive growth in aggregate demand.

    b.   Monetarists believe that the velocity of money is predictable, while Keynesians believe it is unstable.

    c.   Monetarists believe that wages and prices are flexible, while Keynesians do not.

    d.   Monetarists believe that crowding-out negates any positive impact of fiscal policy, while Keynesians see a clear impact of fiscal policy on aggregate demand.

    e.   All of the above.

17.   Most monetarists favor:

    a.   frequent changes in the growth rate of the money supply to avoid inflation.

    b.   placing the Federal Reserve under the Treasury.

    c.   a steady, gradual shrinkage of the money supply.

    d.   none of the above.

18.   Assume the demand for money curve is stationary and the Fed increases the money supply. The result is that people:

    a.   increase the supply of bonds, thus driving up the interest rate.

    b.   increase the supply of bonds, thus driving down the interest rate.

    c.   increase the demand for bonds, thus driving up the interest rate.

    d.   increase the demand for bonds, thus driving down the interest rate.

19.   Keynesians reject the influence of monetary policy on the economy. One argument supporting this Keynesian view is that the:

    a.   money demand curve is horizontal at any interest rate.

    b.   aggregate demand curve is nearly flat.

    c.   investment demand curve is nearly vertical.

    d.   money demand curve is vertical.

20.   Which of the following is *true*?

    a.   Keynesians advocate increasing the money supply during economic recessions but decreasing the money supply during economic expansions.

    b.   Monetarists advocate increasing the money supply by a constant rate year after year.

    c.   Keynesians argue that the crowding-out effect is rather insignificant.

    d.   Monetarists argue that the crowding-out effect is rather large.

    e.   All of the above.

■ TRUE OR FALSE

1. T F John Maynard Keynes listed three types of motives for people holding money—transactions, precautionary, and speculative.

2. T F The opportunity cost of holding money is properly measured by the rate of interest on financial assets such as bonds.

3. T F An increase in the supply of money, other things being equal, will raise the equilibrium interest rate.

4. T F Starting from equilibrium in the money market, suppose the money supply increases. Other things being equal, this will cause an excess demand for money, leading people to sell bonds.

5. T F If the Fed uses its tools to expand the money supply, bond prices will be bid up and interest rates will fall.

6. T F The transmission mechanism is the effect of changes in monetary policy on prices, real GDP, and employment.

7. T F A rightward shift in the money supply curve is likely to produce a rightward shift in the money demand curve.

8. T F Investment is lowered by expansionary monetary policy.

9. T F If the planned-investment curve is relatively flat, the Keynesian conclusion is that the transmission mechanism has little effect on the economy.

10. T F Monetarists argue that the Treasury's conduct of fiscal policy is the most important factor affecting real GDP and interest rates.

■ CROSSWORD PUZZLE

Fill in the crossword puzzle from the list of key concepts. Not all of the concepts are used.

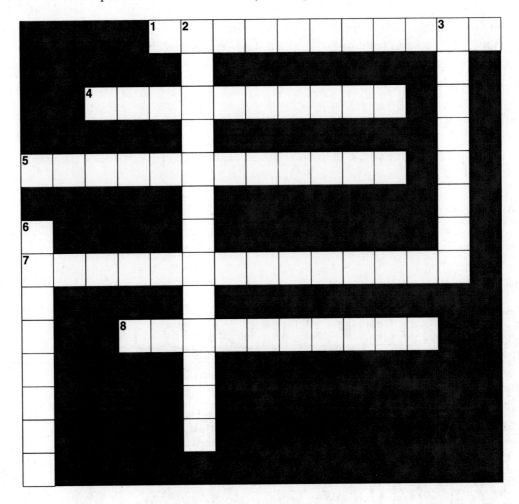

ACROSS

1. _____ demand is money people hold to take advantage of the future price of nonmoney financial assets.
4. The demand for _____ is the quantity of money people hold at different possible interest rates.
5. The _____ demand is money people hold to pay predictable expenses.
7. The _____ _____ of money states that changes in the money supply yield proportionate changes in the price level.
8. The theory that changes in the money supply directly affects the economy.

DOWN

2. The _____ demand is money people hold to pay unpredictable expenses.
3. The _____ of money is the average number of times a dollar is spent.
6. The _____ of exchange is MV=PQ.

■ ANSWERS

Completion Questions

1. transactions demand for money
2. precautionary demand for money
3. speculative demand for money
4. demand for money curve
5. Monetarism
6. equation of exchange
7. velocity of money
8. quantity theory of money

Multiple Choice

1. a 2. c 3. b 4. b 5. e 6. a 7. e 8. b 9. c 10. a 11. a 12. a 13. e 14. e 15. c 16. e 17. d 18. d 19. c 20. e

True or False

1. True 2. True 3. False 4. False 5. True 6. True 7. False 8. False 9. False 10. False

Crossword Puzzle

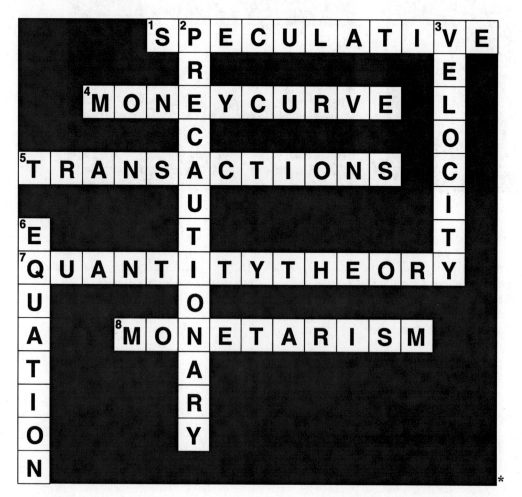

Chapter 20A
Appendix: Policy Disputes Using the Self-Correcting Aggregate Demand and Supply Model

■ CHAPTER IN A NUTSHELL

Using the self-correcting AD/AS model, this appendix explains the disagreement between the classical and Keynesian schools concerning the use of expansionary and contractionary fiscal policy. The classical school advocates nonintervention fiscal and monetary policy. The classical assumption is that flexible nominal wages will cause the short-run aggregate supply curve (SRAS) to shift and automatically restore the economy to long-run full-employment equilibrium. Instead of a passive role, the Keynesian view is that the federal government and Federal Reserve must take an activist role to restore the economy by shifting the aggregate demand supply curve (AD).

■ LEARNING OBJECTIVES

After completing the appendix to this chapter, you should be able to:

1. Explain why the short-run aggregate supply curve is upward sloping.
2. Explain why the long-run aggregate supply curve is vertical.
3. Describe short-run and long run adjustments to changes in aggregate demand on the price level and real GDP.

■ MULTIPLE CHOICE

1. Classical theory advocates _____ policy and Keynesian theory advocates _____ policy.

    a. nonintervention; intervention.
    b. active; nonstabilization.
    c. stabilization; fixed wage.
    d. fixed rule; passive.

2. Assuming the economy is experiencing a recessionary gap, classical economists predict that:

    a. wages will remain fixed.
    b. monetary policy will sell government securities.
    c. higher wages will shift the short-run aggregate supply curve leftward.
    d. lower wages will shift the short-run aggregate supply curve rigthward.
    e. none of the above.

3.   Assume the economy is operating at a real GDP above full-employment real GDP. Keynesian economists would prescribe which of the following policies?

    a. Nonintervention.
    b. Fixed rule.
    c. Contractionary.
    d. Expansionary.

4.   Assume the economy is experiencing an inflationary gap, Keynesian economists would believe that:

    a. flexible wages will restore full employment.
    b. the federal government should decrease spending to shift the aggregate demand curve leftward.
    c. the Federal Reserve should lower the interest rate.
    d. the federal government should increase spending to shift the aggregate demand curve rightward.

Exhibit 1 Macro AD/AS Model

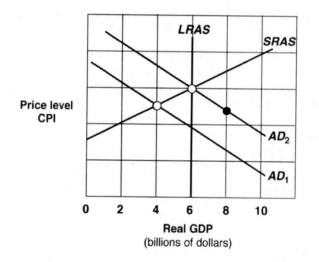

Real GDP
(billions of dollars)

5.   As shown in Exhibit 1, assume the marginal propensity to consume MPC equals 0.75. Using discretionary fiscal policy, federal government spending should be _____ in order to restore the economy to full employment.

    a. increased by $2 trillion.
    b. decreased by $2 trillion.
    c. increased by $.40 trillion.
    d. increased by $.80 trillion.
    e. increased by $1 trillion.

Exhibit 2 Policy Alternative

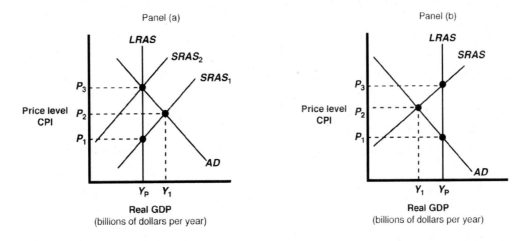

6.   In Panel (a) of Exhibit 2, suppose that the initial equilibrium is at real GDP level Y_1 and price level P_2. At real GDP level Y_1 there is:

    a.   an inflationary gap.
    b.   a recessionary gap.
    c.   full employment.
    d.   long-run equilibrium.

7.   In Panel (a) of Exhibit 2, the economy is initially in short-run equilibrium at real GDP level Y_1 and price level P_2. If the government decides to intervene, it would *most* likely:

    a.   decrease taxes.
    b.   increase transfer payments.
    c.   increase the level of government spending for goods and services.
    d.   decrease the level of government spending for goods and services.

8.   In Panel (a) of Exhibit 2, the economy is initially in short-run equilibrium at real GDP level Y_1 and price level P_2. Classical theory argues that:

    a. $SRAS_1$ will shift to $SRAS_2$ without government intervention.
    b.   lower wages will result in a shift from $SRAS_1$ to $SRAS_2$.
    c.   long-run equilibrium will be established at Y_p and P_3.
    d.   all of the above will take place.

9.   In Panel (b) of Exhibit 2, an expansionary stabilization policy designed to move the economy from Y_1 to Y_p would attempt to shift:

    a.   the aggregate demand curve (AD) leftward.
    b. $SRAS_1$ to $SRAS_2$.
    c.   the aggregate demand curve (AD) rightward.
    d.   the LRAS rightward.

10.   As shown in Panel (b) of Exhibit 2, assume the economy adopts a nonintervention policy. Which of the following would cause the economy to self-correct?

    a. Competition among firms for workers increases the nominal wage and SRAS shifts rightward.

    b. Long-run equilibrium will be established at Y_1 and P_2.

    c. Long-run equilibrium will be established at Y_1 and P_3.

    d. Competition among unemployed workers decreases nominal wages and SRAS shifts rightward.

■ ANSWERS

1. a 2. d 3. c 4. b 5. e 6. a 7. d 8. d 9. c 10. d

PART V
THE INTERNATIONAL ECONOMY

Chapter 21
International Trade and Finance

■ **CHAPTER IN A NUTSHELL**

The purpose of this chapter is to explain why international trade is important. The chapter begins by using the production possibilities curve developed in Chapter 2 to demonstrate that international trade permits specialization, and specialization increases total output for countries. Specialization and trade depend on comparative rather than absolute advantage. Trade can be mutually beneficial even if one country has an absolute advantage in the production of all goods. Embargoes, tariffs, and quotas are barriers to free trade. These forms of protectionism are justified on the basis of the infant industries, national security, employment, cheap labor, and other arguments.

The last part of the chapter explains how a country's balance-of-payments records transactions between nations. The balance of trade refers only to part of the balance of payments. A nation is said to have a favorable balance of trade if its exports of goods exceed its imports of goods. The chapter concludes with an explanation of exchange rates. Assuming a free market for foreign exchange, the exchange rate is determined by the forces of supply and demand.

■ **KEY CONCEPTS**

Absolute advantage	Embargo	World Trade Organization
Appreciation of currency	Exchange rate	(WTO)
Balance of payments	Free trade	
Balance of trade	Protectionism	
Comparative advantage	Quota	
Depreciation of currency	Tariff	

■ **LEARNING OBJECTIVES**

After completing this chapter, you should be able to:

1. Understand that it is mutually beneficial for *all* nations to participate in international trade.
2. Define comparative and absolute advantage and give an example of each.
3. Explain why international trade enables a country to escape the confines of its own production possibilities curve.
4. Explain why trade takes place along the lines of comparative advantage.
5. Describe the various protectionist arguments and explain why an economist would oppose them.

THE ECONOMIST'S TOOL KIT
Applying Supply and Demand to Currencies

Step one: Draw a downward-sloping demand curve for dollars. The vertical axis measures the exchange rate. The fewer the yen per dollar, the greater the quantity of dollars demanded by the Japanese.

Step two: Draw an upward-sloping supply of dollars. The higher the yen per dollar, the greater the quantity of dollars supplied by U.S. citizens.

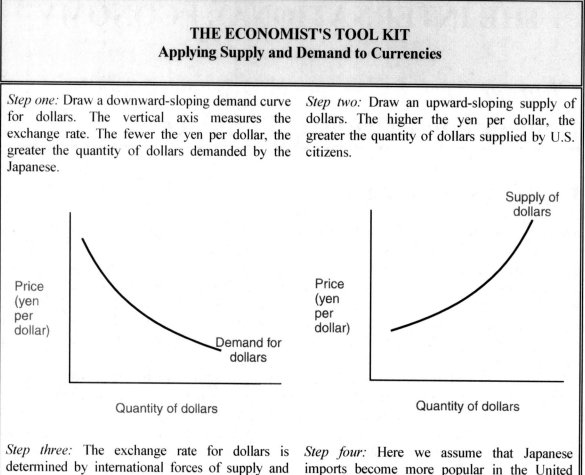

Step three: The exchange rate for dollars is determined by international forces of supply and demand. Suppose some factor, such as a rise in tastes for U.S. exports, increases the demand for dollars from D_1 to D_2. As a result, the value of the dollar rises from P_1^* to P_2^* (dollar appreciates).

Step four: Here we assume that Japanese imports become more popular in the United States. The result is an increase in the supply of dollars from S_1 to S_2. Thus, the value of the dollar falls from P_1^* to P_2^* (dollars depreciate).

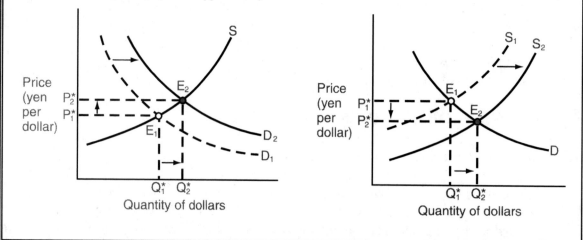

■ COMPLETION QUESTIONS

1. _____ means that each nation specializes in a product for which its opportunity cost is lower in terms of the production of another product and then nations trade.

2. _____ benefits a nation as a whole but individuals may lose jobs and incomes from the competition from foreign goods and services.

3. A government's use of embargoes, tariffs, quotas, and other methods to protect particular domestic industries by imposing barriers that reduce imports is called _____.

4. A (an) _____ prohibits the import or export of particular goods and a (an) _____ discourages imports by making them more expensive. These trade barriers often result primarily from domestic groups that exert political pressure to gain from these barriers.

5. The _____ is a summary bookkeeping record of all the international transactions a country makes during a year. It is divided into different accounts including the current account, the capital account and the statistical discrepancy.

6. The _____ measures only goods (not services) that a nation exports and imports. It is the most widely reported and largest part of the current account.

7. A (an) _____ is the price of one nation's currency in terms of another nation's currency. The intersection of the supply and demand curves for dollars determines the number of units of a foreign currency per dollar.

8. _____ occurs when a currency becomes worth fewer units of another currency and _____ occurs when a currency becomes worth more units of another currency.

9. A _____ is a limit on the quantity of a good that may be imported in a given time period.

■ MULTIPLE CHOICE

1. Trade between nations A and B:

   a. leaves the production possibilities curve of nation A unchanged.
   b. leaves the production possibilities curve of nation B unchanged.
   c. increases the consumption possibilities curves of both nations.
   d. None of the above are true.
   e. All of the above are true.

2.   A country that has a lower opportunity cost of producing a good:

    a.   has a comparative advantage.
    b.   can produce the good using fewer resources than another country.
    c.   requires fewer labor hours to produce the good.
    d.   all of the above.

3.   Which of the following statements is *true*?

    a.   Specialization and trade along the lines of comparative advantage allows nations to consume more than if they were to produce just for themselves.
    b.   Free trade theory suggests that when trade takes place any gains made by one nation comes at the expense of another.
    c.   According to the theory of comparative advantage, a nation should specialize in the production of those goods for which it has an absolute advantage.
    d.   All of the above.

4.   A country that can produce a good using fewer resources than another country has a (an):

    a.   lower opportunity cost of producing the good than another country.
    b.   absolute advantage.
    c.   specialization in the production of the good.
    d.   all of the above.

Exhibit 1 Potatoes and wheat output (tons per day)

Country	Potatoes	Wheat
United States	4	2
Ireland	3	1

5.   In Exhibit 1, the United States has an absolute advantage in producing:

    a.   wheat.
    b.   potatoes.
    c.   both.
    d.   neither.

6.   In Exhibit 1, Ireland's opportunity cost of producing one unit of wheat is:

    a.   1/3 unit of potatoes.
    b.   3 units of potatoes.
    c.   either a or b.
    d.   neither a nor b.

7. In Exhibit 1, the United States has a comparative advantage in producing:

   a. both.
   b. wheat.
   c. potatoes.
   d. neither.

8. If each nation in Exhibit 1 specializes in producing the good for which it has a comparative advantage, then:

   a. the United States would produce potatoes.
   b. the United States would produce both potatoes and wheat.
   c. Ireland would produce neither potatoes or wheat.
   d. Ireland would produce potatoes.

9. Which of the following statements is *true*?

   a. A tariff is a physical limit on the quantity of a good allowed to enter a country.
   b. An embargo is a tax on an imported good.
   c. A quota is a law that bars trade with another country.
   d. When a nation exports more than it imports it is running a balance of trade surplus.

10. Which of the following is *not* an argument used in favor of protectionism?

    a. To protect an "infant" industry.
    b. To protect domestic jobs.
    c. To preserve national security.
    d. To protect against "unfair" competition because of cheap foreign labor.
    e. To reduce prices paid by domestic consumers.

11. If U.S. buyers purchased $500 billion of foreign goods and foreign buyers purchased $400 billion of U.S. goods, the U.S. balance of trade would be:

    a. -$100 billion.
    b. $100 billion.
    c. $400 billion.
    d. none of the above.

12. Which of the following is included in the current account?

    a. Net unilateral transfers.
    b. Goods imports.
    c. Goods exports.
    d. All are included in the current account.
    e. None are included in the current account.

13.   In the U.S. balance of payments, purchases of foreign assets by U.S. residents are tabulated as a (an):

a.   unilateral transfer.
b.   capital outflow.
c.   current account outflow.
d.   capital inflow.

14.   If a Japanese stereo priced at 1,000,000 yen can be purchased for $1,000, the exchange rate is:

a.   1,000 yen per dollar.
b.   1,000 dollars per yen.
c.   .01 dollars per yen.
d.   none of the above.

15.   If the dollar appreciates (becomes stronger) this causes:

a.   the relative price of U.S. goods to increase for foreigners.
b.   the relative price of foreign goods to decrease for Americans.
c.   U.S. exports to fall and U.S. imports to rise.
d.   a balance of trade deficit for the U.S.
e.   all of the above.

16.   An increase in inflation in the United States relative to the rate in France would make:

a.   French goods relatively more expensive in the United States and U.S. goods relatively less expensive in France.
b.   French goods relatively less expensive in the United States and U.S. goods relatively more expensive in France.
c.   French goods relatively more expensive in the United States and in France.
d.   U.S. goods relatively less expensive in the United States and in France.

17.   If there is bilateral currency trade between Japan and the U.S., then as the supply of U.S. dollars on the world foreign exchange market _____, the price of a dollar in terms of Japanese yen will _____.

a.   increases, fall.
b.   decreases, fall.
c.   increases, increases.
d.   decreases, stays the same.

18.   The value of the U.S. dollar in terms of Japanese yen has declined substantially since the mid-1980's. Which of the following would be consistent with that fact?

a.   The supply of yen generated by Japanese buying U.S. goods is low, while the demand for yen generated by U.S. consumers buying Japanese goods is high.

b. The supply of yen generated by Japanese buying U.S. goods is high, while the demand for yen generated by U.S. consumers buying Japanese goods is low.

c. Both the supply of yen and the demand for yen are low because there is relatively little trade between Japan and the U.S.

d. None of the above.

19. If 1 U.S. dollar can be exchanged for 5 euros, then 1 euro can be exchanged for:

    a.   5 cents.
    b.   20 cents.
    c.   50 cents.
    d.   2 dollars.

20. Which of the following would cause the U.S. dollar to depreciate against the Japanese yen?

    a.   Greater popularity of U.S. exports in Japan.
    b.   A higher price level in Japan.
    c.   Higher real interest rates in the United States.
    d.   Higher incomes in the United States.

■ TRUE OR FALSE

1. T   F   A country has a comparative advantage in producing a good when it has the lowest opportunity cost of producing that good.

2. T   F   Absolute advantage governs the potential for gains from trade.

3. T   F   Trade can increase the consumption possibilities of nations.

4. T   F   The current account balance tabulates the value of a country's exports of goods and services minus the value of its imports of goods and services.

5. T   F   A country's imports of goods minus its exports of goods is reported in the merchandise balance.

6. T   F   Other things being equal, an increase in U.S. interest rates would be likely to cause an increase in the capital account surplus or a decrease in the capital account deficit.

7. T   F   Borrowing from foreign banks by U.S. firms represents a capital inflow.

8. T   F   If the current account and capital account are both in surplus, the official reserve account does *not* have to be in deficit.

9. T   F   If the yen price of dollars falls, then the dollar price of yen rises.

10.   T   F   An increase in the price level in Japan relative to the price level in the United States will shift the demand curve for dollars leftward and the dollar depreciates or becomes weaker.

■ CROSSWORD PUZZLE

Fill in the crossword puzzle from the list of key concepts. Not all of the concepts are used.

ACROSS

1.   _____ of currency is a rise in the price of one currency relative to another.
5.   _____ of currency is a fall in the price of one currency relative to another.
7.   The balance of _____ is the value of a nation's imports subtracted from exports.
9.   The _____ rate is the number of units of one nation's money that equals one unit of another nation's money.
10.   A limit on imports.

DOWN

2.   The use of restrictions to protect domestic producers.
3.   A _____ advantage is the ability of a country to produce a good at a lower opportunity cost.
4.   The flow of goods between countries without restrictions or special taxes.
6.   The _____ of payments is a bookkeeping record of all international transactions.
8.   A law that bars trade with another country.

 **ANSWERS**

Completion Questions

1. comparative advantage
2. free trade
3. protectionism
4. embargo, tariff
5. balance of payments
6. balance of trade
7. exchange rate
8. depreciation of currency, appreciation of currency
9. quota

Multiple Choice

1. e 2. a 3. a 4. b 5. c 6. b 7. b 8. d 9. d 10. e 11. a 12. d 13. b 14. a 15. e 16. b 17. a 18. a 19. b 20. d

True or False

1. True 2. False 3. True 4. True 5. False 6. True 7. True 8. False 9. True 10. False

Crossword Puzzle

Chapter 22
Economies in Transition

■ CHAPTER IN A NUTSHELL

The purpose of this final chapter is to explain that pure capitalism and pure communism are polar extremes on a continuum. Most economics are "mixed" and can be classified in reference to one camp or another. The chapter explores the strengths and weaknesses of the three basic types of economic systems including the traditional, command, and market systems. The discussion then turns to the real economic system "isms": capitalism, socialism, and communism. Here, you learn in brief the main ideas of Karl Marx. Also presented in this chapter are of brief discussion of reforms aimed at introducing markets into Cuba, Russia, and China. The chapter ends with a discussion of some of the factors that contribute to the Japanese "malaise".

■ KEY CONCEPTS

Capitalism	Market economy
Command economy	Mixed economy
Communism	Nationalization
Consumer sovereignty	Privatization
Economic system	Socialism
Invisible hand	Traditional economy

■ LEARNING OBJECTIVES

After completing this chapter, you should be able to:

1. Define and describe how the three basic types of economic systems are intended to operate.
2. Describe the strengths and weaknesses associated with the three basic types of economic systems and be able to compare and contrast them.
3. Describe the differences between capitalism, socialism and communism.
4. Understand that *pure* capitalism and *pure* socialism have never existed in the real world.
5. Understand that all real-world economies have both elements of socialism and capitalism present in their systems and that all real-world economies are arrayed between the two extreme dichotomies of pure capitalism and pure socialism depending upon the amount of governmental influence over economic affairs.
6. Explain the pros and cons of government planning.
7. Describe some of the arguments for Japan's success.

■ COMPLETION QUESTIONS

1.   The set of established procedures by which a society answers the What, How, and For Whom to produce goods questions is called a (an) _____.

2.   Three basic types of economic systems are the _____, based on decisions made according to customs, and the _____, which answers the three economic questions through some powerful central authority. In contrast, the _____ uses the impersonal mechanism of the interaction of buyers and sellers through markets to answer the What, How and For Whom questions.

3.   _____ is an economic system in which the factors of production are privately owned, and economic choices are made by consumers and firms in markets.

4.   The determination by consumers of the types and quantities of products that are produced in an economy is called _____.

5.   _____ describes an economy which the government owns the factors of production. The central authorities make the myriad of society's economic decisions according to a national plan.

6.   _____ is an economic system envisioned by Karl Marx to be an ideal society in which the workers own all the factors of production. Marx believed that workers who worked hard would be public spirited and voluntarily redistribute income to those who are less productive.

7.   A phrase that expresses the belief that the best interests of a society are served when individual consumers and producers compete to achieve their own private interests is called a (an) _____.

8.   A _____ is an economic system that answers the What, How, and For Whom questions through a mixture of traditional, command, and market systems.

■ MULTIPLE CHOICE

1.   Which of the following is a basic question by an economic system?

   a.   for whom goods and services are produced.
   b.   how goods and services are produced.
   c.   what goods and services are produced.
   d.   all of the above.
   e.   none of the above.

2.   An economic system that answers the What, How, and For Whom questions using prices determined by the interaction of the forces of supply and demand is a:

   a.   market economy.
   b.   command economy.
   c.   tradtional economy.
   d.   none of the above.

3.   An economic system characterized by private ownership of the factor of production and economic activity coordinated through a system of markets and prices is called:

   a.   capitalism.
   b.   socialism.
   c.   communism.
   d.   none of the above.

4.   Adam Smith's book The Wealth of Nations was published at the time of the:

   a.   Great Depression.
   b.   U.S. Declaration of Independence.
   c.   U.S. Civil War.
   d.   War of 1812.

5.   What famous economist said that the market economy seemed to be controlled by an invisible hand?

   a.   Alfred Marshall.
   b.   Adam Smith.
   c.   Karl Marx.
   d.   Robert L. Heilbroner.

6.   Which of the following is *true* in a market economy?

   a.   Central planners determine answers to the basic economic questions.
   b.   Resources are used efficiently.
   c.   The distribution of wealth is equal.
   d.   Information for production and distribution decisions pass directly to buyers from the government.

7.   Which of the following statements is *true*?

   a.   The doctrine of laissez-faire advocates an economic system with extensive government intervention and little individual decision-making.
   b.   In capitalism income is distributed on the basis of need.
   c.   Adam Smith was the father of socialism.
   d.   Most real-world economies are mixed economic systems.
   e.   The "invisible hand" refers to government economic control.

8.   Which of the following is a characteristic of capitalism?

    a.   Government ownership of all capital.
    b.   Government decision-making is preferred to decentralized decision-making.
    c.   Market determination of prices and quantity.
    d.   Equality of income.

9.   Socialism is correctly described by which of the following statements?

    a.   Central planning is used exclusively to answer the basic economic questions.
    b.   Markets are used exclusively to answer the basic economic questions.
    c.   Tradition answers the basic economic questions.
    d.   Government ownership of many resources and centralized decision-making answers the basic economic questions.

10.   Which of the following is a characteristic of socialism?

    a.   Rejection of central planning.
    b.   Government ownership of all factors of production.
    c.   Government ownership of most of the factors of production.
    d.   Private ownership of all factors of production.

11.   Which of the following statements is *true*?

    a.   The United States today comes closer to the socialist form of economic organization than it does capitalism.
    b.   When central planners set prices above equilibrium for goods and services they create shortages.
    c.   According to Karl Marx, under capitalism, workers would be exploited and would revolt against the owners of capital.
    d.   Adam Smith argued that government's role in society would be to do absolutely nothing.

12.   In Japan, the government agency that combines government and businesses in joint ventures is called.

    a.   MITI.
    b.   GOSPLAN.
    c.   JEEOC.
    d.   KEIRETSU.

13.   Which of the following is *not* an idea advocated by Adam Smith?

a.   Businessmen conspiring to fix prices is a threat to the price system.
b.   Pursuit of private self interest with an "invisible hand" is the best way to promote the public interest.
c.   Government should control the control the economy with an "invisible hand".
d.   The government should provide for national defense and little else.

14.   In Adam Smith's competitive market economy, the question of what goods to produce is determined by:

a.   the "invisible hand" of the price system.
b.   businesses.
c.   unions.
d.   the government, through laws and regulations.

15.   Karl Marx was a (an):

a.   19th century German philosopher.
b.   18th century Russian economist.
c.   14th century Polish banker.
d.   19th century Russian journalist.

16.   Who was one of the first proponents of employing market economies instead of command economies?

a.   Robert Heilbroner.
b.   Karl Marx.
c.   Jeffrey Sachs.
d.   Adam Smith.

17.   What type of economic system is commonly described as being controlled by an "invisible hand"?

a.   A traditional economy.
b.   A command economy.
c.   A market economy.
d.   A communist economy.

18.   Who predicted that the exploitation of workers would cause capitalism to self-destruct?

a.   Milton Friedman.
b.   Robert Heilbroner.
c.   Karl Marx.
d.   Adam Smith.

19.   Which of the following is one common criticism of capitalism?

    a.   Poor product quality and little product diversity.
    b.   Inefficiency of nationalized industries.
    c.   Inability to adjust quickly to changing economic conditions.
    d.   Inadequate environmental protection.

20.   Socialism is an economic system characterized by:

    a.   private ownership of resources and market decision-making.
    b.   government ownership of resources and centralized decision-making.
    c.   cooperation, sharing, and little central government.
    d.   a complex structure of rules and traditions that dictates decision-making.

■ TRUE OR FALSE

1.   T   F   A traditional system solves basic economic questions by long-standing customs.

2.   T   F   A traditional system operates based on the self-interest of buyers and sellers.

3.   T   F   A command system uses a group of planners or central authority to make basic economic decisions.

4.   T   F   The command system relies on prices set by firms on the basis of consumer demands.

5.   T   F   When the official price for goods and services is below the equilibrium price in a market, prices no longer perform their rationing function efficiently.

6.   T   F   Adam Smith believed that a nation would produce the maximum wealth by relying on government to make public interest economic decisions.

7.   T   F   A market system does not operate based on self-interest.

8.   T   F   In the real world, countries use a mixture of the three basic types of economic systems.

9.   T   F   Under socialism, no markets can operate at all.

10. T   F   Karl Marx viewed socialism only as a transition to the ideal state of communism.

11. T   F   In Marx's ideal state of communism there would be no haves and have-nots.

■ CROSSWORD PUZZLE

Fill in the crossword puzzle from the list of key concepts. Not all concepts are used.

ACROSS

4. An economic system characterized by private ownership.
6. A _____ economy is a system where a central authority answers the basic economic questions.
7. A phrase that expresses the belief that the best interests of a society are served when individual consumers and producers compete to achieve their own private interests.
8. A _____ economy is a mix of traditional, command, and market systems.
9. A _____ economy is a system that answers the basic economic questions the way they have always been answered.

DOWN

1. A stateless, classless economic system envisioned by Karl Marx as the ideal society.
2. An economic system characterized by government ownership of resources and centralized decision-making.
3. The way society organizes to answer the basic economic questions.
5. Consumer _____ is the freedom of consumers to cast their dollar votes in markets.

■ ANSWERS

Completion Questions

1. economic system
2. traditional economy, command economy, market economy
3. capitalism
4. consumer sovereignty
5. socialism
6. communism
7. invisible hand
8. mixed economy

Multiple Choice

1. d 2. a 3. a 4. b 5. b 6. b 7. d 8. c 9. d 10. c 11. c 12. a 13. c 14. a 15. a 16. d 17. c 18. c 19. d 20. b

True or False

1. True 2. False 3. True 4. False 5. True 6. False 7. False 8. True 9. False 10. True 11. True

Crossword Puzzle

Chapter 23
Growth and the Less-Developed Countries

■ CHAPTER IN A NUTSHELL

Economic growth and economic development are related, but somewhat different, concepts. Growth is measured quantitatively by GDP per capita. Development includes GDP per capita but also incorporates quality-of-life measures such as life expectancy, literacy rates, and per capita energy consumption.

Growth and development are a result of a complex process that is determined by five major factors: (1) natural resources, (2) human resources, (3) capital, (4) technological progress, and (5) the political environment. Although there is no single correct strategy for economic growth and development, the experience of the "Four Tigers of the Pacific Rim" (sometimes called the "Asian Tigers") might suggest what might be necessary.

GDP per capita provides a general index of a country's standard of living. GDP per capita comparisons are subject to four problems: (1) The accuracy of LDC data is questionable, (2) GDP ignores the degree of income distribution, (3) Changes in exchange rates affect gaps between countries, and (4) there is no adjustment for the differences in cost of living between countries.

Unlike industrially advanced nations (IACs), less developed countries (LDCs) have a low GDP per capita and output is produced without large amounts of technologically advanced capital and well-educated labor. The LDCs account for three-fourths of the world's population.

The "vicious circle of poverty" is a trap in which the LDC is too poor to save money and therefore it cannot invest enough to significantly increase its production possibilities. As a result the LDC remains poor. Consequently, many LDCs are looking for external sources of funds in the form of foreign private investment, foreign aid, and foreign loans.

■ KEY CONCEPTS

Agency for International Development
Foreign aid
GDP per capita
Industrially advanced countries (IACs)
Infrastructure

International Monetary Fund
Less developed countries (LDCs)
New International Economic Order
Vicious circle of poverty
World Bank

■ LEARNING OBJECTIVES

After completing this chapter, you should be able to:

1. Define GDP per capita and describe why an increase is desirable.
2. Describe the characteristics of industrially advanced countries (IACs) and less developed countries (LDCs), and contrast the differences between them.
3. Describe the four problems of comparing GDP per capita data for different countries.
4. Explain the similarities and difference between economic growth and development.

5.   Describe the five major factors that determine economic growth and development.
6.   List the "Four Tigers of the Pacific Rim" and suggest what may have given rise to their success as newly industrialized countries in the world.
7.   Describe what is meant by the term "vicious circle of poverty" as the term is used to explain why poor countries have such a difficult time growing and developing.
8.   Describe some external sources of funds to less developed nations and the potential role of the World Bank and the International Monetary Fund (IMF).

■ COMPLETION QUESTIONS

1.   _____ is the value of final goods produced (GDP) divided by the total population.

2.   High-income nations which have market economies based on large stocks of technologically advanced capital and well-educated labor are called _____.

3.   _____ are nations without large stocks of technologically advanced capital and well-educated labor. LDCs are economies based on agriculture such as most countries of Africa, Asia, and Latin America.

4.   The _____ is a trap in which countries are poor because they cannot afford to save and invest, but they cannot save and invest because they are poor.

5.   Capital goods usually provided by the government, including highways, bridges, waste and water systems, and airports are called _____.

6.   _____ is the transfer of money or resources from one government to another for which no repayment is required.

7.   The agency of the U.S. State Department that is in charge of U.S. aid to foreign countries is called _____.

8.   The _____ is the lending agency that makes long-term low-interest loans and provides technical assistance to less-developed countries.

9.   The _____ is the lending agency that makes short-term conditional low-interest loans to developing countries.

10.   A series of proposals made by LDCs calling for changes that would accelerate the economic growth and development of the LDCs is called _____.

■ MULTIPLE CHOICE

1.   According to the classification in the text, which of the following is *not* an IAC?

   a.   New Zealand.
   b.   Russia.
   c.   United Arab Emirates.
   d.   All of the above are IACs.

2.   The number of countries of the world classified as LDCs is:

   a.   25.
   b.   50.
   c.   75.
   d.   150.
   e.   250.

3.   According to the classification in the text, which of the following is *not* a LDC?

   a.   Hong Kong.
   b.   Israel.
   c.   Argentina.
   d.   Greece.

4.   Which of the following is a problem when comparing GDPs per capita between nations?

   a.   GDP per capita is subject to greater measurements errors for LDCs compared to IACs.
   b.   Fluctuations in exchange rates effect differences in GDP per capita.
   c.   GDP per capita fails to measure income distribution.
   d.   All of the above.
   e.   None of the above.

5.   Which of the following is *not* generally considered to be an ingredient for economic growth?

   a.   Investment in human capital.
   b.   Political instability.
   c.   High savings rate and investment in capital.
   d.   Growth in technology.
   e.   Investment in infrastructure.

6.   Which of the following statements is *true*?

a.   A less developed country (LDC) is a country with a low GDP per capita, low levels of capital, and uneducated workers.
b.   The vicious circle of poverty exists because GDP must rise before people can save and invest.
c.   LDCs are characterized by rapid population growth and low levels of investment in human capital.
d.   All of the above.

7.   Countries are poor because they cannot afford to save and invest is called the:

a.   vicious circle of poverty.
b.   savings-investment trap.
c.   LDC trap.
d.   cycle of insufficient credit.

8.   Which of the following is infrastructure?

a.   Police.
b.   Training and education.
c.   Highways.
d.   All of the above.
e.   None of the above.

9.   Which of the following statements is *true*?

a.   There is no single correct strategy for economic growth and development.
b.   In general, GDP per capita is highly correlated with alternative quality of life measures.
c.   The "New International Economic Order" is a set of proposals by LDCs that would give them greater control over the policies of international financial institutions.
d.   All of the above.

10.   Which of the following is true concerning GDP per capita comparisons?

a.   The accuracy of LDC GDP per capita data is questionable.
b.   GDP per capita ignores the degree of income distribution.
c.   GDP per capita is affected by exchange rate changes.
d.   GDP per capita does not account for the difference in the cost of living among nations.
e.   All of the above are true.

11.   International comparisons of per-capita GDP may not reflect standard of living because
_____.

    a. Currency exchange rates may not fully account for differences in purchasing power, and thus people in a country with high per-capita GDP may have a lower standard of living because of high local prices for food, housing, or other necessities.
    b. People in some countries enjoy poverty and do not mind a lack of access to medicine, education, nutritious food, and safe drinking water.
    c. Markets do not exist in less-developed countries.
    d. None of the above.

12.   Which of the following *best* describes the cycle of poverty?

    a. Rich countries eventually decline because is citizens become lazy.
    b. Poor countries eventually improve through investment in education, infrastructure, and capital accumulation.
    c. Rich countries stay rich through continued high levels of investment in education, infrastructure, and capital accumulation.
    d. Poor countries stay poor because they cannot afford to invest in education, infrastructure, and capital accumulation.

13.   Which of the following is an example of a multilateral lending agency that makes loans, rather than gifts of foreign aid, to less-developed countries?

    a. The Agency for International Development.
    b. The International Red Cross.
    c. The World Bank.
    d. Church World Relief.

14.   Which of the following is *not* a common characteristic of industrially advanced countries (IACs)?

    a. Market-based economies.
    b. Large stocks of technologically advanced capital.
    c. Well-educated labor.
    d. Low per capita energy consumption.

15.   The poorest regions in the world, as measured by GDP per capita, are:

    a. Latin America and the Caribbean.
    b. the Middle East and North Africa.
    c. Sub-Saharan Africa and South Asia.
    d. Australia and New Zealand.

16.   GDP per capita is a relatively good measurement of:

   a.   the distribution of income.
   b.   purchasing power.
   c.   household production.
   d.   the standard of living.

17.   Which of the following can be a barrier to an LDC's economic growth and development?

   a.   Low population growth.
   b.   A low level of human capital.
   c.   Faster capital accumulation.
   d.   More infrastructure.

18.   Capital goods provided by the government such as roads, airports, and water systems make up the country's:

   a.   supply of capital.
   b.   infrastructure.
   c.   standard of living.
   d.   political environment.

19.   Which of the following makes short-term, conditional loans to developing countries?

   a.   The Agency for International Development (AID).
   b.   The World Bank.
   c.   The North American Free Trade Agreement (NAFTA).
   d.   The International Monetary Fund (IMF).

20.   The "Four Tigers" of East Asia are the newly industrialized countries of Taiwan, South Korea, Hong Kong, and:

   a.   Japan.
   b.   Singapore.
   c.   The Phillippines.
   d.   Vietnam.

■ TRUE OR FALSE

1.   T   F   A country with a high GDP per capita is classified as an IAC.

2.   T   F   According to the text, Singapore is classified as a LDC.

3.   T   F   According to the text, Ireland and Israel are classified as IACs.

4.   T   F   In general, GDP per capita is not highly correlated with alternative measures of quality of life.

5.   T   F   A country can develop without a large natural resource base.

6.   T   F   The vicious circle of poverty is the trap in which the LDC is too poor to save and therefore it cannot invest and remains poor.

7.   T   F   The Agency for International Development is the agency of the U.S. State Department that is in charge of U.S. aid to foreign countries.

8.   T   F   The main purpose of the International Monetary Fund is to manage and distribute U.S. foreign aid.

9.   T   F   The world bank is the agency of the U.S. State Department that is in charge of U.S. loans to foreign countries.

■ CROSSWORD PUZZLE

Fill in the crossword puzzle from the list of key concepts. Not all of the concepts are used.

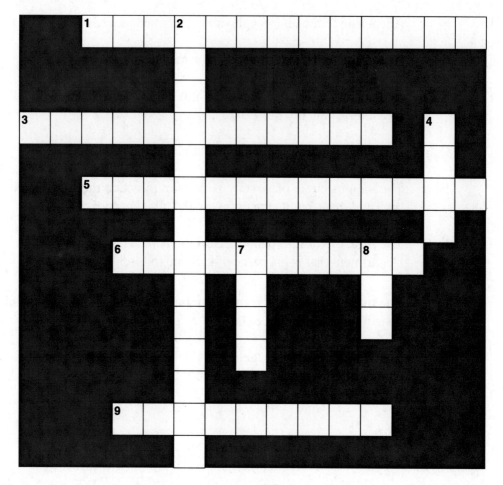

ACROSS

1. _____ of poverty is the trap in which countries are poor because they cannot afford to save and invest, but they cannot save and invest because they are poor.
3. The value of final goods produced (GDP) divided by the total population.
5. _____ countries are nations without large stocks of technologically advanced capital and well-educated labor.
6. The transfer of money or resources from one government to another for which no repayment is required.
9. The lending agency that makes long-term low-interest loans and provides technical assistance to less-developed countries.

DOWN

2. Capital goods usually provided by the government, including highways, bridges, waste and water systems, and airports.
4. A series of proposals made by LDCs calling for changes that would accelerate the economic growth and development of the LDCs.
7. High-income nations that have market economies based on large stocks of technologically advanced capital and well-educated labor.
8. The lending agency that makes short-term conditional low-interest loans to developing countries.

ANSWERS

Completion Questions
1. GDP per capita
2. industrially advanced countries (IACs)
3. less-developed countries (LDCs)
4. vicious circle of poverty
5. infrastructure
6. foreign aid
7. Agency for International Development
8. World Bank
9. International Monetary Fund
10. New International Economic Order

Multiple Choice

1. c 2. d 3. a 4. d 5. b 6. d 7. a 8. c 9. d 10. e 11. a 12. d 13. c 14. d 15. c 16. d 17. b 18. b 19. d 20. b

True or False

1. True 2. False 3. True 4. False 5. True 6. True 7. True 8. False 9. False

Crossword Puzzle

CPSIA information can be obtained
at www.ICGtesting.com
Printed in the USA
FFOW03n2234190814
6971FF